Youness Manzali
Faiq Gmira
Mohamed ELFAR

RESEARCH ADVANCES IN MACHINE LEARNING

Youness Manzali
Faiq Gmira
Mohamed ELFAR

RESEARCH ADVANCES IN MACHINE LEARNING

TREES, KNN, AND CLUSTERING MODELS

Noor Publishing

Imprint
Any brand names and product names mentioned in this book are subject to trademark, brand or patent protection and are trademarks or registered trademarks of their respective holders. The use of brand names, product names, common names, trade names, product descriptions etc. even without a particular marking in this work is in no way to be construed to mean that such names may be regarded as unrestricted in respect of trademark and brand protection legislation and could thus be used by anyone.

Cover image: www.ingimage.com

Publisher:
Noor Publishing
is a trademark of
Dodo Books Indian Ocean Ltd. and OmniScriptum S.R.L publishing group

120 High Road, East Finchley, London, N2 9ED, United Kingdom
Str. Armeneasca 28/1, office 1, Chisinau MD-2012, Republic of Moldova, Europe
Managing Directors: Ieva Konstantinova, Victoria Ursu
info@omniscriptum.com

Printed at: see last page
ISBN: 978-620-9-37947-5

Abstract

Machine Learning is a powerful approach for extracting valuable insights and building analytical models from data with minimal human intervention. With the ever-growing volume and variety of data, choosing the most suitable algorithm for a specific dataset poses a significant challenge. This book introduces innovative methods to enhance existing machine learning algorithms through advanced data analysis techniques, addressing key issues in classification, ensemble learning, and clustering. The first proposal is based on the decision tree algorithm, where improvements include a novel pre-pruning technique that halts node creation based on probability thresholds. Additionally, a new method is proposed to reinforce weak nodes in decision trees by augmenting data from similar nodes, enhancing overall model performance. In the realm of random forests, this book presents a pruning strategy that uses association rule metrics to optimize branch selection, resulting in improved predictive accuracy. Furthermore, a hybrid algorithm combining Random Forest and Naive Bayes is developed, demonstrating superior performance in forecasting student outcomes across different datasets. For K-nearest neighbors (KNN) algorithms, a feature weighting technique is introduced, integrating association rules and information gain to prioritize influential attributes in the dataset. An enhanced KNN method is also proposed, employing ensemble learning and correlation-based feature subset selection, achieving notable performance improvements over traditional approaches. Finally, this work presents a novel clustering approach that leverages frequent itemset mining and a combined distance measure. By using frequent patterns and maximizing the dissimilarity between cluster centers, this technique offers a more effective and efficient way to group data. Our proposed methods are evaluated using a consistent experimental framework applied to widely recognized, publicly available machine learning datasets from platforms such as the UCI Repository and Kaggle. The experimental results validate the effectiveness of these contributions, which represent significant advancements in machine learning by introducing new tools and methodologies to address diverse challenges in data analysis.

Keywords: Machine Learning, classification algorithm, ensemble technique, clustering, data-mining, artificial intelligence.

ملخص

يُعد التعلم الآلي منهجًا قويًا لاستخلاص معلومات قيمة وبناء نماذج تحليلية من البيانات مع تدخل بشري محدود. ومع النمو المستمر في حجم وتنوع البيانات، يصبح اختيار الخوارزمية الأنسب لمجموعة بيانات معينة تحديًا كبيرًا. تقدم هذه الأطروحة للدكتوراه منهجيات مبتكرة لتحسين الخوارزميات الحالية للتعلم الآلي من خلال تقنيات متقدمة لتحليل البيانات، مع التركيز على معالجة الاشكاليات الرئيسية المتعلقة بالتصنيف، وتقنيات التجميع، وخوارزميات التجميع.

تتمثل أولى المساهمات في تحسين خوارزمية أشجار القرار من خلال تطوير تقنية جديدة للتقليم المسبق تعتمد على عتبات احتمالية لإيقاف إنشاء العقد. بالإضافة إلى ذلك، تم اقتراح طريقة جديدة لتعزيز العقد الضعيفة في أشجار القرار من خلال زيادة البيانات من عقد مشابهة، مما يحسن من أداء النموذج بشكل عام.

فيما يتعلق بالغابات العشوائية، تقدم الأطروحة استراتيجية تقليم تعتمد على مقاييس مستمدة من قواعد الارتباط لتحسين اختيار الفروع، مما يؤدي إلى تحسين دقة التنبؤات. علاوة على ذلك، تم تطوير خوارزمية هجينة تجمع بين الغابات العشوائية وخوارزمية نايف بايز، وأظهرت نتائج متميزة في توقع أداء الطلاب على مجموعات بيانات مختلفة.

بالنسبة لخوارزميات أقرب الجيران (KNN) ، تم تقديم تقنية جديدة لتحديد أوزان الميزات تعتمد على قواعد الارتباط ومكاسب المعلومات، بهدف إعطاء الأولوية للسمات الأكثر تأثيرًا في مجموعة البيانات. كما تم اقتراح منهجية محسّنة لهذه الخوارزمية تعتمد على التعلم التجميعي واختيار مجموعة فرعية من السمات بناءً على الارتباط، مما حقق تحسينات ملحوظة مقارنة بالنهج التقليدية.

أخيرًا، تقترح هذه الدراسة طريقة مبتكرة للتجميع تعتمد على استخراج الأنماط المتكررة وقياس مسافة مركّب. من خلال استخدام الأنماط المتكررة وزيادة التباين بين مراكز المجموعات، توفر هذه الطريقة نهجًا أكثر كفاءة وفعالية لتجميع البيانات.

تم تقييم المنهجيات المقترحة باستخدام إطار تجريبي متسق على مجموعات بيانات معترف بها. أثبتت النتائج التجريبية فعالية هذه المساهمات، التي تمثل تقدمًا كبيرًا في مجال التعلم الآلي من خلال تقديم أدوات ومنهجيات جديدة لمعالجة التحديات المتنوعة لتحليل البيانات.

الكلمات المفتاحية: التعلم الآلي، خوارزميات التصنيف، تقنيات التجميع، التكتل، استخراج البيانات، الذكاء الاصطناعي.

Contents

List of Figures

List of Tables

List of Abbreviations

AI	Artificial Intelligence
CART	Classification And Regression Trees
CFI	Clustering using Frequent Item sets
DAGs	Directed Acyclic Graphs
DL	Deep Learning
DM	Data Mining
DT	Decision Tree
EKNN	Ensemble of K Nearest Neighbor
EM	Ensemble Methods
EPMID	Equal Predictability Merging for Incremental Decision Trees
FE	Feature Extraction
FS	Feature Selection
FW	Feature Weighting
HOT	Hoeffding Option Trees
ID3	Iterative Dichotomiser 3
KDD	Knowledge Didcovery in Data
KNN	K Nearest Neighbor
ML	Machine Learning
NB	Naive Bayes
NRF	Noisy Random Forest
PR	Pattern Recognition
RF	Random Forest
RFCNB	Random Forest Combined with Naive Bayes
RS	Random Subspace
SVM	Support Vector Machine
WKNN	Weighted K Nearest Neighbor

Introduction

Context

In recent years, machine learning (ML) has emerged as a transformative technology, driving advancements across various domains, including healthcare, finance, transportation, and environmental science. Its ability to analyze vast amounts of data and uncover patterns has enabled the development of predictive models, automation systems, and decision-support tools that were previously inconceivable. As society increasingly relies on data-driven solutions, the demand for more efficient, accurate, and scalable ML algorithms has grown significantly.

Despite the remarkable progress in machine learning, several challenges persist (Figure 1). Standard ML algorithms often struggle with issues such as high computational complexity, poor generalization to unseen data, and susceptibility to noisy or imbalanced datasets. Furthermore, the practical deployment of ML models requires careful consideration of factors such as interpretability, robustness, and adaptability to dynamic environments. Addressing these challenges is critical for ensuring that machine learning systems deliver reliable and impactful solutions in real-world applications.

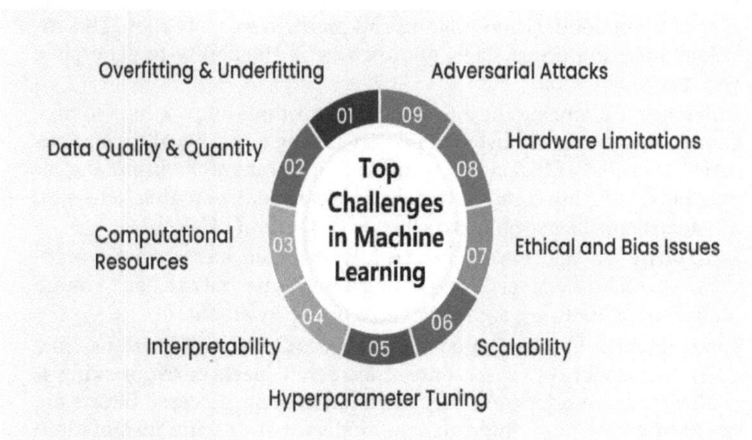

FIGURE 1 – Challenges in Machine Learning.

This book is motivated by the need to enhance the capabilities of machine learning algorithms to better meet the demands of diverse and complex problems. By focusing on improving the core aspects of ML algorithms—including their efficiency, accuracy, and robustness—this work aims to bridge the gap between theoretical advancements and practical implementations. Additionally, this book explores novel applications of these enhanced algorithms in key areas where traditional approaches have proven insufficient or inefficient.

The dual focus on improvement and application provides a holistic perspective on advancing machine learning research. On one hand, algorithmic enhancements contribute to the foundational understanding and utility of ML techniques. On the other, their application to real-world problems demonstrates the tangible benefits of these improvements, highlighting their potential to address pressing societal and industrial challenges. Through this synergy, the book seeks to contribute both to the theoretical development of machine learning and its practical impact.

Motivation

Improving machine learning algorithms is an iterative process, involving research, experimentation, and validation. The collective efforts in this area lead to advancements that drive the widespread adoption of machine learning across various industries and applications. The main reasons for improving machine learning algorithms are basically the following:

- **Accuracy**: Improving the accuracy of machine learning algorithms is crucial for better decision-making and predictive capabilities. This involves reducing errors, bias, and increasing the ability to generalize well to unseen data.
- **Efficiency**: Enhancing the efficiency of algorithms allows them to process and analyze data faster, making real-time or near-real-time applications feasible. Efficiency improvements can involve optimizing algorithms, reducing computational complexity, or leveraging hardware advancements like specialized chips (e.g., GPUs, TPUs).
- **Scalability**: As data sizes grow rapidly, it becomes essential for algorithms to scale effectively. Developing algorithms that can handle large datasets efficiently is a significant area of improvement.
- **Interpretability**: Many modern machine learning algorithms, like deep neural networks, are often considered black boxes, making it challenging to understand their decision-making process. Efforts are made to create more interpretable models that provide insights into how and why specific predictions are made.
- **Robustness**: Machine learning algorithms should be robust to noise, outliers, and adversarial attacks. Improving robustness ensures that models perform consistently under different conditions.

- **Data efficiency**: Training machine learning models often requires large amounts of labeled data. Algorithms that can achieve good performance with smaller datasets are desirable, as labeling data is time-consuming and expensive.
- **Generalization**: Generalization refers to a model's ability to perform well on new, unseen data from the same distribution as the training data. Improving generalization helps models avoid overfitting and ensures adaptability to various scenarios.
- **Transfer learning**: This area focuses on improving algorithms by leveraging knowledge gained from one task or domain to improve performance on another related task or domain.
- **Online learning**: Algorithms that can learn incrementally from streaming data or adapt in real-time are vital in dynamic and changing environments.
- **Ethical considerations**: As machine learning algorithms become more powerful, ensuring their fairness, transparency, and ethical use is a critical aspect of improvement.

The main findings of this book

This book primarily centers around the research of machine learning algorithms and their application to high-dimensional and classification datasets. The primary findings of this book, aimed at addressing the aforementioned challenging issues through the development of novel machine learning algorithms, are succinctly outlined in the following sequence:

1. **Organizing the state-of-the-art of machine learning algorithms**: The book begins by meticulously organizing the current state-of-the-art in machine learning algorithms. This serves to provide the reader with a comprehensive and structured overview of the field.
2. **Critical Analysis**: A critical and empirical evaluation of existing machine learning algorithms is conducted. This analysis not only supplements insights into the strengths and weaknesses of these methods but also offers valuable recommendations to aid researchers and enlighten readers.
3. **Novel Algorithms**: The book introduces innovative machine learning algorithms designed to tackle the challenge of reducing the model complexity and execution time of a given problem. These novel algorithms are engineered with the goal of either maintaining or enhancing the performance of existing learning algorithms.
4. **Benchmarking Platform**: The book creates a robust benchmarking platform for the comparative assessment of various machine learning methods. This platform facilitates the systematic evaluation and comparison of different algorithms, providing a basis for informed decision-making in practical applications.

In this book, the primary attention is directed toward machine learning algorithms, specifically delving into their operational principles, as well as a comprehensive examination of the pros and cons of each algorithm. These aspects are elucidated and individually exemplified in the subsequent key concepts:

Analyzing the state of the art of machine learning algorithms.

Our objective is to compile the latest advancements in machine learning algorithms, aiming to create a comprehensive and informative overview that benefits our readers. Furthermore, we intend to conduct a thorough assessment of the performance of the most widely used machine learning methods. This evaluation will be empirical, involving multiple benchmark datasets, allowing us to uncover their strengths, weaknesses, and practical suitability.

Developing new machine learning methods

The second section of this book is dedicated to the introduction of novel machine learning techniques designed to overcome the limitations of existing methods while maintaining efficiency. A total of seven foundational machine learning approaches will be presented.

This dissertation's main finding is the introduction of new machine-learning algorithms that eliminate the drawbacks of the existing ones. The research performed for this book resulted in the following:

The **first research** direction we approach in supervised learning is the problem of pre-pruning in the decision tree algorithm. In this work, we developpe a new pre-pruning algorithm that stops the tree creation when the node probability is high (above a certain threshold). This prevents the tree from overfitting the training data too precisely and allows it to generalize better to new data. The second research on decision trees introduces a new algorithm that reinforces weak nodes in a tree by increasing its data from similar tree nodes. We have used two approaches to calculate the similarity between two nodes.
The **second part** of the contributions concerns the pruning of the random forest algorithm, The third research presents a new algorithm that extracts branches from the built forest, then validates them using association rules metrics by considering each branch as an association rule where the attributes and conditions encountered along the branches can be seen as the antecedents of the association rules, and the class labels assigned to the leaf nodes can be considered as the consequent. Finally, we remove less important branches, making the built model less complex and less likely to memorize noise in the training data. This improves the model's ability to generalize to new, unseen data. The second research in this direction is very similar to the previous one since it also prunes the forest branches, but it uses Naive Bayes posterior probability to evaluate the branches, and it applies this technique to two student performance datasets.
The **third direction** of treats the K-Nearest Neighbors(KNN) algorithm. In the first work, we propose a new KNN feature weighting approach that applies association rules and information Gain. The second research is about KNN ensemble methods; it proposes a new KNN ensemble method

that uses correlation to select feature subsets for each estimator.

The **final area of research** focuses on clustering algorithms. In this study, we introduce a novel clustering approach called the CFI algorithm (Clustering using Frequent Item Sets), which relies on frequency rather than distance. This method utilizes frequent item sets to construct clusters. To achieve this, we combine a similarity measure with Euclidean distance, creating a fused distance. The proposed distance is maximized to determine the centroids of the clusters. Through various experiments, the superiority of the CFI algorithm is demonstrated.

Structure

The structure of the book chapters follows a logical and cohesive progression, resembling a ladder-like arrangement. This organization ensures a smooth and interconnected flow between the existing and newly proposed machine learning methods. It provides the reader with a comprehensive overview of the essential key points emphasized in this book, allowing for a holistic understanding of the subject matter.

- The **chapter** 1 serves as the gateway to our book, where we introduce, contextualize, and highlight the machine-learning problems we'll be addressing. It also lays out the essential definitions and concepts necessary for a deep understanding of machine learning intricacies, forming the foundational structure of our research. Additionally, Chapter 1 dissects and elucidates the entire machine-learning process. Initially, it delves into the significant challenges that have garnered attention. Subsequently, this chapter provides detailed descriptions of the key machine-learning algorithms employed in our book. This serves as a fundamental starting point and preliminary groundwork, offering both readers and researchers a foundational understanding of the machine-learning landscape.
- The **chapter** 2 **Modified decision trees** proposes two modified decision trees algorithms. The first introduces a new pre-pruning algorithm, while the second propose a new decision tree algorithm that enhances weak nodes by increasing its data from similar nodes

- The **chapter** 3 **random forest pruning methods** proposes two random forest pruning techniques. The first uses association rules metrics to prune branches. The second contribution uses Naives Bayes posterior probability and applied to two student performance datasets

- The **chapter** 4 **Improved version of KNN** introduces two modified KNN algorithms. The first one presents a new feature weighting for KNN based on association rules and information gain. The second study suggests a new KNN ensemble method based on feature correlation.

- The **chapter 5 A New Frequency-Based Clustering Algorithm** introduces a new clustering algorithm that uses frequent items sets and a fused distance measure to build cluster centroids.

- **Conclusion and Future Work**: As to the last chapter, we conclude the book by summarizing the main concepts, topics, findings, and the attained results. Moreover, we suggest some recommendations for researchers as well as providing some perspectives in relation to machine learning algorithms.
- **Publications of the Author**: Publications of the Author contains publications of the author that are related to this book work.

Chapter 1

Background & Literature Overview

Contents

This chapter serves as an introduction to the fundamental concepts underpinning each stage of the machine learning process utilized in this dissertation. It encompasses the data and methodologies employed to develop models and formulate hypotheses. Additionally, the chapter delves into the various approaches accessible for evaluating the constructed models. To be more specific, it provides an overview of the contemporary data generation possibilities and the existing learning techniques.

1.1 Introduction to machine learning

Machine learning algorithms have revolutionized the way we process information and make decisions in the modern world. At its core, machine learning involves creating intelligent systems that can automatically learn and improve from experience without being explicitly programmed. These algorithms enable computers to recognize patterns, make predictions, and uncover valuable insights from vast amounts of data.

The applications of machine learning span across various fields, driving innovations and enhancing efficiency in industries such as healthcare, finance, marketing, and more (Figure 1.1). From image and speech recognition to natural language processing and recommendation systems, machine learning plays a pivotal role in powering intelligent technologies that impact our daily lives.

In this exploration, we will delve into the workings of machine learning algorithms, understanding their underlying principles and how they contribute to solving complex problems across diverse domains. By grasping the potential of these algorithms, we can unlock new possibilities and embrace a future where intelligent machines continue to shape and augment human endeavors.

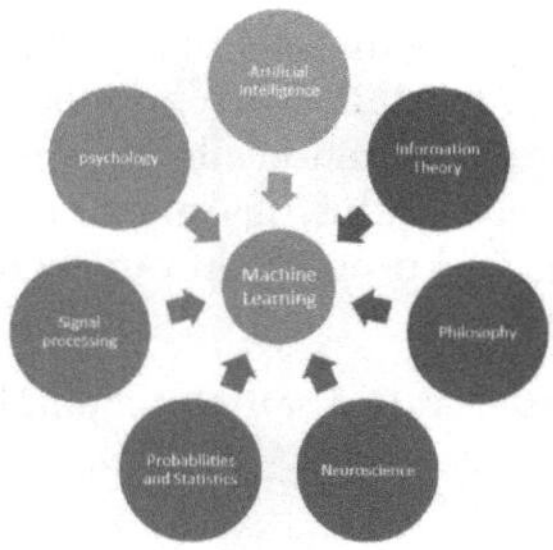

FIGURE 1.1 – The Multi-disciplinary Machine learning.

1.2 Data

As the foundation of any machine learning model, data plays a pivotal role in shaping its performance and accuracy (Figure 1.2). It is a well-established principle that the more data we have at our disposal, the more robust and precise the model becomes. This is because larger datasets provide a richer and more diverse set of patterns and examples for the model to learn from.

FIGURE 1.2 – architecture of a decision model.

When a model is trained on a vast and varied dataset, it gains a deeper understanding of the underlying patterns and relationships within the data. This allows the model to generalize better to unseen data, making it more adept at making accurate predictions and informed decisions.

Moreover, abundant data helps the model capture nuances and complexities that might otherwise be missed with limited data. It enhances the model's ability to handle edge cases and challenging scenarios, making it more reliable and trustworthy in real-world applications.

Having an accurate model is crucial for enabling good decisions. In fields like healthcare, finance, and autonomous systems, precise predictions can be the difference between success and failure, life and death. A well-trained model based on extensive data can significantly increase confidence in the decisions made by the system, providing valuable insights and aiding in critical decision-making processes.

However, it is essential to note that data quality also matters significantly. Clean, relevant, and unbiased data is vital for building a reliable model. If the data used for training is of poor quality or contains biases, it can lead to inaccurate and potentially harmful decisions.

In conclusion, the availability of extensive and high-quality data is a cornerstone of building accurate machine-learning models. Emphasizing the importance of data collection and curation allows us to develop models that have a positive impact on various industries and domains, empowering better decision-making and driving progress in our increasingly data-driven world.

In Machine Learning, the data is called samples. Samples are often noted as a vector:

$$x = (x_1, x_2, ..., x_p) \tag{1.1}$$

Where p is the number of attributes.

1.2.1 Data type

There are two main families of data:

- **Labeled data**: A group of samples that have been accompanied by one or more labels. These labels are used to identify the decision to be made for each sample. It is often costly (time and money) to have large volumes of labeled data.
- **Non-labeled data**: labels do not accompany the data. Even if unlabeled data is more challenging to use, it is much more accessible. (An interesting example is retrieving millions of images from the web for face recognition).

1.2.2 Target type

We distinguish two types of output y as shown in Figure 1.3:

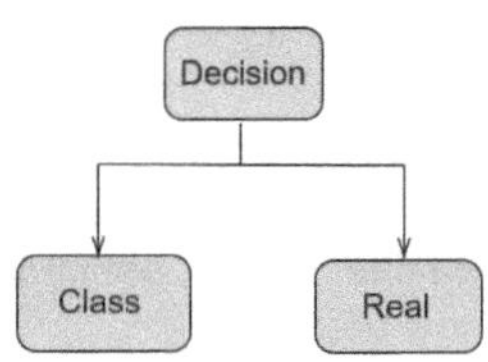

FIGURE 1.3 – Example of a target type for a decision mode.

- **Categorized or discrete labels**: the number of values that can take y is finite. In this case, the possible outputs are called classes. In general, for C classes, we can say that:

  $$y \in \{1, 2, ..., C\} \tag{1.2}$$

  Where y, is an integer that varies between 1 and C.

- **Uncategorized or continuous labels**: the number of values that y can take is infinite. In general, We can see the model as a function noted f, which takes an input sample and returns a decision.

Discretization empowers data handling by converting continuous variables into distinct categories, enabling more efficient processing and analysis.

1.2.3 Discretization

Data discretization is a crucial preprocessing step in many data analysis and machine learning tasks. It involves transforming continuous data into discrete intervals or bins, which simplifies the data representation and makes it more manageable for analysis. By partitioning the data into intervals, we can reduce the effects of outliers and noise while preserving the essential patterns and trends in the dataset. This process not only facilitates easier interpretation but also enables the use of various algorithms that require discrete data as input. Overall, data discretization plays a fundamental role in enhancing the efficiency and accuracy of data-driven models and decision-making processes. This operation is often carried out to simplify a representation or to project towards a form of the variable suited to the type of processing desired.

A machine learning algorithm can be mathematically represented as a function f, where x denotes the input data, and y represents the corresponding output or prediction as shown in Figure 1.4. The function f encapsulates the learned mapping from the input space to the output space, capturing the underlying patterns or relationships in the data. Depending on the type of learning task, f can represent a wide variety of models, such as linear regression, decision trees, neural networks, or support vector machines, each tailored to address specific problems and optimize performance metrics.

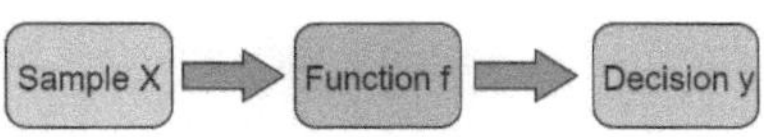

FIGURE 1.4 – A machine learning algorithm, expressed as a function f with input x, output y.

The determination of f is the heart of a Machine Learning problem. It takes place in two stages:

1. Choice of a generic function.
2. Determination of function parameters using samples. This phase is called model training or learning.

1.3 Learning approaches

Machine learning methods can be categorized into several groups, depending on their intended objectives and adopted approaches.

1.3.1 Supervised Learning

Supervised learning is a method that aims to predict the class of new instances based on prior information. It involves two main steps: a learning step and a classification step. In the learning step, a model is constructed by analyzing a "learning" dataset, where each instance's class is predefined. Let $D = \{(X_i; Y_i); i \in \{1; ...; N\}\}$ be the training dataset containing N instances. Each instance $(X_i, \{X_i^1, \ldots, X_i^d\}, Y_i \in \{1; ...; J\})$ is represented by a vector of d-dimensional variables and a target variable Y_i, indicating its membership in one of the J classes. We define χ and κ as the spaces of input and output values, respectively. Formally, during the learning stage, the goal is to learn a function $f : \chi \rightarrow \kappa$ from the learning data, such that $f(X)$ serves as a "good" predictor for the corresponding value of Y. In the classification step, the model built in the first stage is used to classify new instances. It is essential for the learning algorithm's model to meet various criteria. As an illustrative example, let's consider:

- The primary objective of supervised learning is to minimize the error rate, aiming for the highest accuracy possible. This can be evaluated using various criteria such as precision (ACC), area under the ROC curve (AUC), Log loss (LOG), and others.
- The model should be robust and less affected by random fluctuations in the training data, ensuring consistent performance across different datasets.
- An essential aspect of supervised learning is to make classification decisions as explicit and interpretable as possible, facilitating understanding and insights into the model's predictions.

Regarding the types of supervised learning, they are classified based on the nature of the variable to predict:

- **Classification**: When the target variable is qualitative or categorical, the task involves classifying instances into predefined classes or categories. The goal is to find a decision boundary separating the different classes in the feature space.
- **Regression**: In contrast, when the target variable is quantitative or numerical, the objective is to predict a continuous value. Here, the model aims to learn the underlying relationship between input features and the numerical output, allowing it to make predictions for unseen data points.

1.3.2 Unsupervised Learning

The Unsupervised Learning system (Barlow, 1989) aims to identify groups of individuals with shared characteristics by discovering patterns and relationships in the dataset through clustering. "Clustering" methods, also known as "regrouping," all share the same objective: determining an optimal grouping of observations based on defined criteria to create distinct classes of individuals. In practice, "clustering" can be used for typology or segmentation tasks. The optimization of partitioning involves seeking homogeneity within each class and heterogeneity between classes, grouping similar individuals together while achieving maximum dissimilarity between classes.

One prominent example of unsupervised learning is K-means (MacQueen et al., 1967), a simple method of aggregation around mobile centers. This algorithm employs a dynamic reallocation of individuals to class centers, which are recalculated at each iteration. The data is treated as a vector representation of observations in $\mathbb{R}^p$ with a metric, typically the Euclidean distance, measuring the distance between points in the p-dimensional space. The iterative process of K-means involves two steps:

1. Assign each individual to the class whose center is closest based on the Euclidean distance.
2. Calculate the coordinates of the k centers for the formed classes.

To assess the quality of the unsupervised learning or clustering results, a metric is required for the space. The Euclidean distance is the most common choice. Two types of indicators are calculated using this metric:

- Inter-class inertia: Measures the distance between different groups obtained.
- Intra-class inertia: Measures the proximity of individuals belonging to the same group.

The selection of the best clustering approach involves finding a balance between these two types of indicators. Therefore, numerous other indicators have been proposed in the literature, computed from the inter-class and intra-class inertias. (Malika et al., 2014) provides details about the most common indicators used for this purpose.

1.3.3 Reinforcement learning

Reinforcement learning (Sutton et al., 1998) is a learning approach where an agent interacts with its environment and learns by observing the outcomes of its actions. The goal is for the agent to determine the optimal behavior in a specific context to maximize its performance. This learning process relies on feedback, referred to as the reward signal, which guides the agent in learning how to act effectively.

The concept of reinforcement learning mirrors the way humans and animals learn. We perform actions and observe their consequences in our environment, a fundamental aspect known as "cause and effect" that underpins our knowledge accumulation throughout life.

The core idea of reinforcement learning lies in the agent's ability to interact with the environment and learn from the outcomes of its actions. It follows a trial-and-error approach, where the agent receives rewards for correct actions and penalties for incorrect ones. Based on the accumulated rewards, the agent refines its behavior through training. Once trained, the agent can predict how to act in response to new data presented to it.

The process of "cause and effect" in reinforcement learning can be described in the following steps:

1. The agent observes an initial state.
2. A decision-making function (policy) determines the action to be taken.
3. The agent performs the chosen action.
4. The environment provides feedback in the form of a result or reward based on the action taken.
5. Information about the result for this state-action pair is recorded.

The agent can learn the best actions to take in different states by repeatedly performing them and observing the resulting rewards.

The ultimate goal is for the agent to gather sufficient observations across states, leading to the generation of an optimal decision policy. This policy enables the machine to act perfectly within that specific environment. Unlike other forms of machine learning, the machine does not know in advance which actions or decisions to take; it must explore and discover the actions that yield the highest rewards through trial and error.

In more complex scenarios, actions may influence not only immediate rewards but also subsequent situations and, consequently, all future rewards. This makes reinforcement learning particularly intriguing and powerful in situations where actions have long-term consequences.

1.3.4 Semi-supervised Learning

Semi-supervised learning bridges the gap between unsupervised learning and supervised learning by using a large number of unlabeled data during the training process. It falls under the category of weak supervision. Leveraging unlabeled data can significantly enhance learning accuracy, especially when only a small amount of labeled data is available.

In many learning problems, obtaining labeled data often requires the involvement of skilled human agents or physical experiences, making the labeling process costly and impractical for large training sets. On the other hand, acquiring unlabeled data is relatively inexpensive. In such scenarios, semi-supervised learning becomes highly valuable. It not only has practical applications but also holds theoretical significance for machine learning and serves as a model for human learning.

Semi-supervised learning deals with a dataset containing both identically and independently distributed examples with corresponding labels and unlabeled examples. By combining this information, semi-supervised learning can outperform the classification performance achieved by either discarding unlabeled data and performing supervised learning or ignoring labels and performing unsupervised learning.

There are two main types of semi-supervised learning:

1. Transductive Learning: The focus is on inferring correct labels for the unlabeled data provided. In analogy, one can think of the learning problem as an exam, and the labeled data acts as examples of problems solved by the teacher to help solve another set of problems represented by the unlabeled data. In the transductive framework, the unlabeled data serves as the unresolved examination questions.
2. Inductive Learning: The goal is to predict labels for unseen or new data points. In this case, the unlabeled data represents practical problems that will be encountered in the future, similar to those that will constitute the examination.

Semi-supervised learning offers a powerful approach to getting the most out of both labeled and unlabeled data, enabling more accurate and cost-effective solutions for learning problems in various domains.

1.4 Classification

In the field of machine learning, classification refers to the task of determining the category to which a new observation belongs based on its similarities with previously analyzed data for which the category of membership is known. A more formal definition of classification is as follows:

Definition Given a set of data points $X = x_1, ..., x_n$, each belonging to a finite set of classes $Y = y_1, ..., y_m$, the classification task involves generating a function $f : X \rightarrow Y$ that maps elements of X to their corresponding classes in Y.

Each data point x_i is commonly referred to as an instance or sample and is characterized by a finite set of features $F = f_1, ..., f_m$, which can be either categorical or numerical. These features are also known as attributes or variables; in this context, the terms will be used interchangeably. Each data point x_i is associated with a label y_i that indicates its class from the finite set Y. The ultimate goal is to develop a model that, given a data point x_i, can accurately determine its corresponding label y_i.

The classification process involves two main phases: model creation and model usage. In the model construction phase, the objective is to build a model that can effectively "explain" the underlying concept represented by the data. This model is trained using a set of labeled data representing the target concept. In the model usage phase, the trained model is employed to classify future unlabeled samples, assigning them to the appropriate classes based on what it has learned from the training data (Figure 1.5).

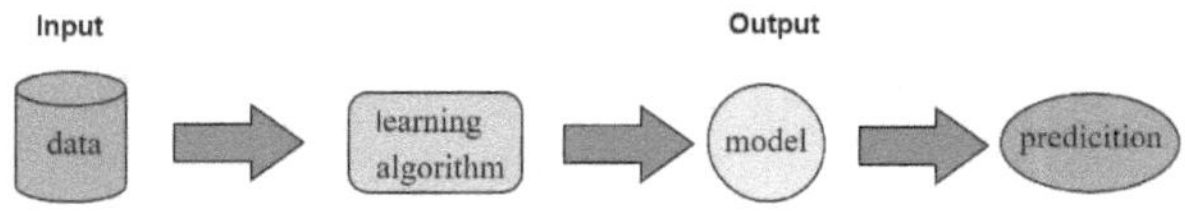

FIGURE 1.5 – Classification as the task of generating a model to map the input features into class labels.

Developing a model that can generalize well and capture the underlying concept represented by the instances is essential, rather than merely memorizing or reproducing the training data itself. Generalization ensures that the model can accurately classify new, unseen data, making it a valuable tool for various real-world applications. If the learning system fails to capture and generalize the underlying data concept, it will result in a significant generalization error. In other words, when faced with new, unseen instances, the system will likely misclassify them. However, since future instances are unavailable during the model-building process, simulating the model usage phase becomes essential. By simulating the model's performance on future data, we can determine the success of the learning process and estimate its future generalization error rate.

The available data is divided into two sets to conduct this simulation: the training set and the test set. The model is first generated by learning from the labeled training set, allowing it to grasp the underlying patterns in the data. Subsequently, the test set is used to evaluate whether the model accurately identifies the concept represented by the input data. If the learning algorithm has effectively constructed a robust model, the instances in the test set will be classified correctly.

This simulation of model usage is a fundamental step in machine learning. It provides valuable insights into the model's performance when presented with new, real-world data. Moreover, it helps in detecting overfitting, where the model memorizes the training data but fails to generalize effectively to new instances. An illustration of the model usage simulation is depicted in Figure 1.6. The evaluation of a model involves determining how accurately it can predict the labels of test instances that were not seen during the learning phase. In other words, the model's performance is assessed based on how well it can generalize to new and unseen data.

1.5 Regression

Regression is used to establish the relationship between one or more input variables (features) and a numeric output variable. The primary goal of regression is to predict or estimate a continuous output value based on the values of the input attributes.

For instance, in the context of predicting house prices, the regression model would analyze various features such as the area of the house, the number

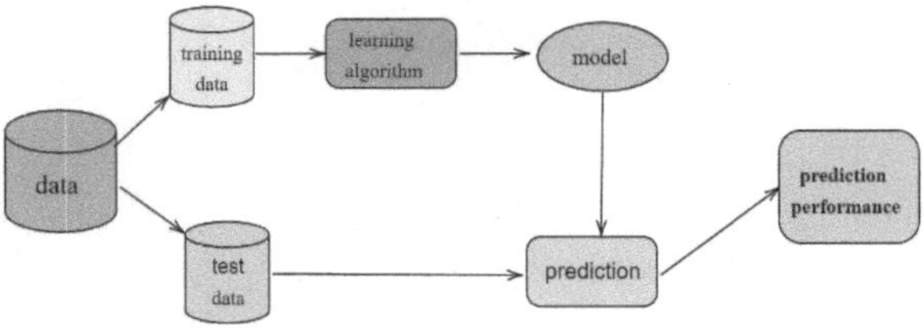

FIGURE 1.6 – The general approach to build and validate a predictive model.

of floors, the location, and other relevant attributes and then estimate the house's price based on these factors.

During the training phase, the regression model learns from labeled data, including input-output pairs. The model aims to find a computational function that best fits the training data and can accurately predict the output value for new, unseen input data.

Regression models come in various forms, such as linear regression, polynomial regression, and support vector regression, among others. Each type of regression model tries to find the optimal relationship between the input features and the numeric output, allowing for precise predictions in real-world applications.

1.5.1 Linear regression

Linear regression (Montgomery, 1982) stands as one of the most widely used supervised learning algorithms and is renowned for its simplicity and well-established understanding in both statistics and machine learning.

At its core, linear regression serves as a fundamental predictive analysis tool, addressing two key questions:

Can a set of predictor variables effectively predict an outcome variable? Which variables exert the most significant influence on the outcome variable? These regression estimates help explain the relationship between a dependent variable and one or more independent variables. The simplest form of the regression equation, known as simple linear regression, involves a single dependent variable (y) and a single independent variable (x). This is represented as $y = c + b \times x$, where c represents the constant term, b is the regression coefficient, and x denotes the independent variable (Figure 1.7).

For more complex scenarios, such as multiple linear regression, where there are multiple independent variables (x_1 to x_n), the equation expands to $y = c+b\times x_1+...+n\times x_n$, where b up to n are the respective regression coefficients associated with each independent variable.

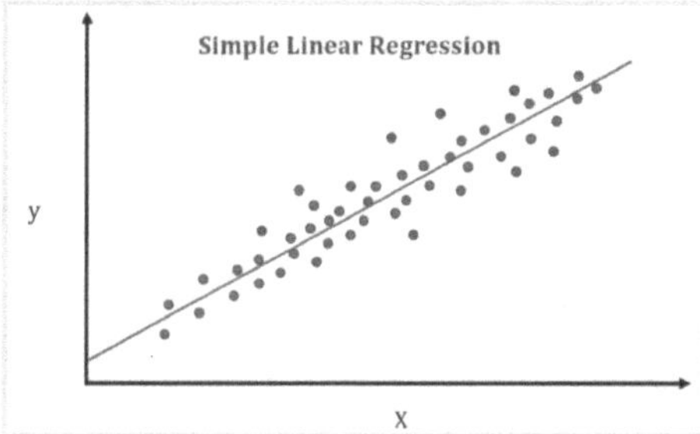

FIGURE 1.7 – Example of a two dimensional representation of the equation where the x axis refers to an input and the y refers to the output. Source: Benjamin Obi Tayo

1.5.2 Logistic regression

Linear regression predicts continuous values, such as temperatures in degrees, whereas logistic regression (Wright, 1995) predicts discrete values, specifically a finite set of values like true or false. Logistic regression is particularly well-suited for binary classification tasks. For example, consider a dataset where the target variable y can only take the values 0 or 1, where 1 represents the positive class (e.g., rain) and 0 represents the negative class (e.g., no rain).

In the context of logistic regression, unlike linear regression, the predicted output is expressed as probabilities of belonging to the positive class. These probabilities fall within the interval $[0, 1]$ since they represent the likelihood of the positive class occurrence. The logistic function $h(x) = \frac{1}{1+e^{-x}}$ transforms the input value x into a probability value within this range (Figure 1.8).

After obtaining the probability, a threshold is applied to convert the probability into a binary classification decision. For instance, if the probability exceeds a certain threshold (often set to 0.5), the output is assigned to the positive class (1); otherwise, it is assigned to the negative class (0).

This makes logistic regression particularly valuable for tasks where we want to predict a binary outcome, such as whether an event will occur or not, based on the input features. The logistic regression model outputs probabilities, which can then be converted into discrete predictions using a predefined threshold.

1.6 Clustering

Clustering is a method used to categorize objects into meaningful subgroups called clusters, based on their distance or similarity. Each cluster is composed of similar objects, while objects from different clusters are dissimilar. Various techniques for clustering have been developed, falling into two main

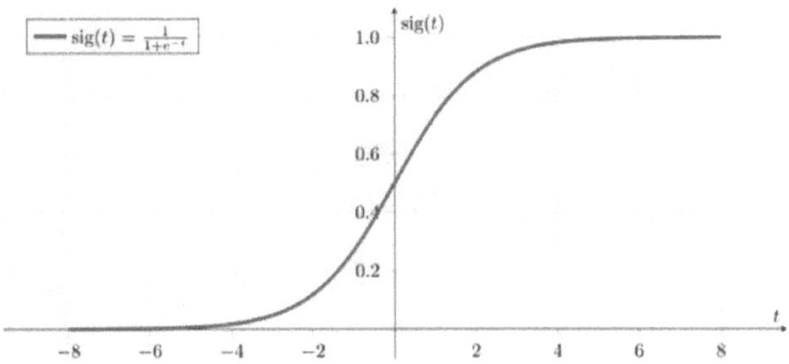

FIGURE 1.8 – Logistic Regression plot (falls within the legitimate range of 0 to 1)

categories: partitional and hierarchical. The K-means algorithm is particularly notable due to its simplicity and efficiency.

1.6.1 Partitional Clustering

Partitional clustering involves dividing a dataset into clusters so that objects within the same cluster are more alike than those in different clusters. For a strict partition, two conditions must be met: every cluster must have at least one object, and each object should belong to just one cluster. However, exhaustively searching all possible partitions for global optimization can be extremely time-consuming.

The widely used K-means algorithm (MacQueen, 1967), belonging to partitional clustering, takes a different approach. It segments a dataset into homogeneous and compact clusters designated by 'k'. The process starts with the random assignment of 'k' centers and labels (0, 1, ..., k). Then, distances from each point to the 'k' centers are calculated, and each point is assigned to the nearest center and label. New centers are computed as gravity centers for labeled points, and this iteration continues until centers stabilize. A key feature of K-means is the placement of a circle (or hypersphere in higher dimensions) centered on each cluster, with a radius based on the farthest cluster point. However, K-means works best for circular data distributions, as depicted in Figure 1.9. For non-circular data shapes, K-means might not yield appropriate results, as illustrated in Figure 1.10.

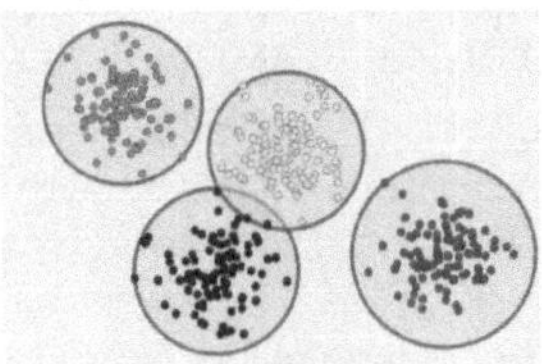

FIGURE 1.9 – A simple example showing how K-Means Clustering works efficiently when the data is circular.

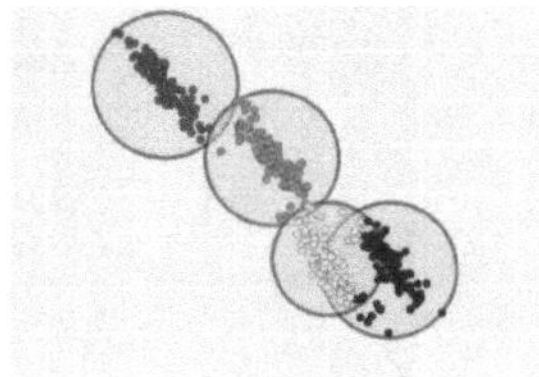

FIGURE 1.10 – An example of when k-means is not the appropriate clustering method.

To address data shapes beyond circles, the Gaussian mixture model (McLachlan and Basford, 1988) was introduced. It accommodates elongated clusters by considering variation, which is reflected in the width of the bell-shaped curve. The distribution's shape in two dimensions is determined by variance or covariance, as shown in Figure 1.11. Standard clustering algorithms encounter performance and quality issues with large datasets. BIRCH (Balanced Iterative Reducing and Clustering using Hierarchies) (Zhang et al., 1996) offers a solution by creating a condensed dataset summary that retains crucial information.

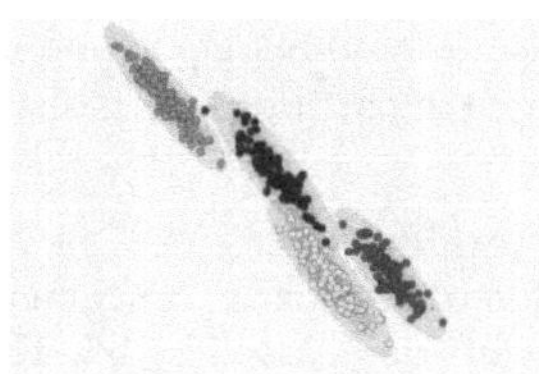

FIGURE 1.11 – An example shows the case when the Gaussian mixture is more suitable than K-means.

Extensions to K-means include K-prototypes (Huang, 1997a) and K-modes (Huang, 1997b) for specific data types. K-prototypes handles mixed data types, while K-modes is suitable for categorical data.

1.6.2 Hierarchical Clustering:

Hierarchical clustering arranges clusters in a hierarchy. Two primary categories are agglomerative and divisive hierarchical clustering.

- Agglomerative (Kurita, 1991): This type proceeds bottom-up, merging clusters as it ascends. A prominent method here is Ward's agglomerative clustering (Xu and Tian, 2015), which aggregates data points based on their similarities.
- Divisive: This top-down strategy recursively divides the hierarchy after combining all observations into one group.

Hierarchical clustering results are often represented through dendrograms. Techniques like Single-link clustering (S-link) (Sibson, 1973), Complete-link clustering (C-link) (Defays, 1977), and Average-link clustering (A-link) (Olson, 1995) are utilized.

- S-link method (Sibson, 1973): It's an agglomerative approach, joining clusters by pairing the closest elements from different clusters.
- C-link method (Defays, 1977): Also agglomerative, this method fuses the two farthest clusters in each stage.
- A-link method (Olson, 1995): It calculates the average distance between clusters based on their elements.

1.7 Association rules

Association rules are a helpful approach for finding relevant relations in huge data sets. It was first used to analyze market basket data to discover patterns in product sales that might aid retailers in discovering new chances for cross-selling to clients. The origin of the association rules dates back to the AIS algorithm (Agrawal et al., 1993) proposed by R. Agrawal in 1993. The AIS method does not use the frequent itemsets attribute since it generates many candidate itemsets. The frequent itemsets concept was subsequently introduced by R. Agrawal and R. Srikant, who also introduced the Apriori algorithm (Agrawal et al., 1994), a critical method that is currently frequently used in business. Several searches were drawn to the topic of mining association rules due to Apriori, and many enhanced algorithms were presented, including the Apriori-Hybrid algorithm (Agrawal et al., 1994), the fuzzy association rule algorithm (Kuok et al., 1998), and the FP-Growth algorithm (Han et al., 2000).

1.7.1 Support and Confidence

An association rule is an implication expression of the form $X \to Y$, where X and Y are separate itemsets. The relevance of an association rule is measured by some metrics, such as support and confidence (Mining, 2006). The frequency of items in Y appearing in instances that contain X is determined by confidence. In contrast, the applicability of a rule to a particular data set is determined by support. These measurements' official definitions are:

$$support(X \to Y) = \frac{frq(X \bigcup Y)}{N} \tag{1.3}$$

$$confidence(X \to Y) = \frac{frq(X \bigcup Y)}{frq(Y)} \tag{1.4}$$

1.7.2 Lift

In addition to the support-confidence metrics for association rules, lift is a correlation metric. If $P(X,Y) = P(X)P(Y)$, then the occurrence of itemset X is independent of the occurrence of itemset Y. If not, the events for itemsets X and Y are dependent and connected. More than two itemsets can be included in this definition with ease. Computing may determine the lift between the incidence of X and Y.

$$lift(X,Y) = \frac{P(X \bigcup Y)}{P(X)P(Y)} \tag{1.5}$$

If the $lift(X,Y)$ is smaller than 1, the incidence of X is inversely related to the occurrence of Y. If the $Lift(X,Y)$ is larger than 1; this implies that X and Y are positively related, which means that the occurrence of one excludes the occurrence of the other; if the $Lift(X,Y) = 1$, X and Y are independent and there is no relation between them (Mining, 2006).

1.7.3 Apriori algorithm

The Apriori method was the first association rules mining algorithm to systematically manage the explosive growth of candidate itemsets through support-based pruning. The operating process of Apriori can be divided into two main stages: The initial stage consists of Iteratively identifying all frequent itemsets with supports greater than the user-defined threshold.

The second stage is to create association rules using frequent itemsets that fulfill the user-defined minimal confidence. Let FI_k be a frequent itemset, where $FI_k = \{i_1, i_2, \ldots, i_k\}$. The following method may be used to build association rules for this itemset: The first rule is $\{i_1, i_2, ..., i_k - 1\} \rightarrow i_k$. By examining the confidence, it is possible to decide whether or not this rule is interesting. The final items in the antecedent are then deleted and added to the consequence to create new rules. The confidences of the new rules are then tested to see whether they are interesting. These procedures repeated themselves up until the antecedent was empty (Mining, 2006).

1.8 K-Nearest Neighbors

The k-Nearest Neighbors (k-NN) algorithm (Hart et al., 2000) is a simple and intuitive machine learning algorithm used for both classification and regression tasks. It operates on the principle of similarity and assumes that data points that are close to each other in feature space are likely to belong to the same class or have similar output values. Here's a brief overview of how the k-NN algorithm works:

1.8.1 Data and Training Phase:

The algorithm is provided with a labeled dataset consisting of input feature vectors and their corresponding class labels (for classification) or output values (for regression). During the training phase, the algorithm stores the entire training dataset in memory for reference during prediction.

1.8.2 Prediction Phase:

When given a new, unlabeled input data point, the k-NN algorithm calculates the distance (e.g., Euclidean distance (Eq.1.6)) between this input point and all the points in the training dataset. The algorithm then selects the k nearest neighbors based on the smallest calculated distances. "k" is a user-defined parameter that determines the number of neighbors to consider. For classification tasks, the algorithm assigns the class label that is most frequent among the k neighbors to the new input point. This label is often determined by a majority vote among the neighbors. For regression tasks, the algorithm calculates the average or weighted average of the output values of the k neighbors and assigns this as the predicted value for the new input point.

$$d(x,y) = \sqrt{\sum_{i=1}^{n}(x_i - y_i)^2} \tag{1.6}$$

Where:

n represents the number of dimensions (features) in the data.
x_i and y_i are the corresponding feature values of the two data points being compared.

1.8.3 Choosing the Optimal k:

The choice of the parameter "k" is important and can significantly impact the performance of the algorithm. A small value of "k" might result in noise affecting predictions, while a large value might lead to over-smoothing. Selecting the optimal value for "k" can often be determined through techniques like cross-validation.

1.8.4 Advantages and Considerations:

k-NN is simple to understand, requires minimal training effort, and can capture complex decision boundaries. It works well when the data has clear separation between classes or when local patterns are important. However, it can be computationally expensive during prediction, especially for large datasets, as it needs to compute distances for all training examples. The algorithm's effectiveness may diminish when dealing with high-dimensional data, as the notion of "nearest neighbors" becomes less meaningful.

1.8.5 Distance Metrics:

The choice of distance metric (e.g., Euclidean distance, Manhattan distance) can impact the algorithm's performance, and it should be chosen based on the nature of the data and the problem.

In the provided illustration (Fig 1.12), we've set the value of 'K' to 3. This signifies that the algorithm examines the three nearest neighbors to the new data point to determine its classification. The proximity between data points is evaluated using metrics like Euclidean distance (Equation 1.7). With 'K'

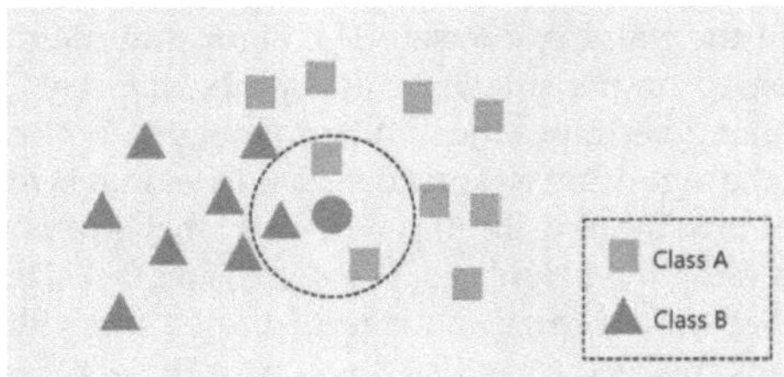

FIGURE 1.12 – Example illustrating How does KNN Algorithm work?

set at 3, the neighboring points consist of two squares and one triangle. Consequently, if we were to classify the new data point under 'K' = 3, it would be categorized as Class A (squares).

1.9 k-Nearest Neighbor Ensembles

The use of the k-Nearest Neighbor (k-NN) algorithm as a base learner within ensemble techniques can be traced back to at least 2000, when (Domingos and Hulten, 2000) introduced an innovative ensemble approach for k-Nearest Neighbor classification. In their work, the authors outline a methodology for employing multiple k-NN classifiers within an ensemble framework. Each of these classifiers is trained on a randomly selected subset of the training data. Subsequently, the predictions generated by these individual classifiers are aggregated using a weighted voting mechanism, culminating in the ultimate classification decision. Through empirical illustrations, the authors validate that their approach enhances the accuracy of k-NN classification across various datasets. Furthermore, they conduct a comparative analysis of their technique vis-à-vis alternative ensemble methods like bagging and boosting. Various researchers have explored the efficacy of k-Nearest Neighbor (k-NN) ensemble methods in diverse applications. (Kumutha and Palaniammal, 2013) propose an advanced method for handling missing data by combining bagging and k-Nearest Neighbor (k-NN) imputation techniques. By training multiple k-NN imputers on bootstrapped data subsets, the approach aims to enhance imputation accuracy and reliability. This fusion of bagging and k-NN addresses missing values more effectively, improving dataset integrity. (Ajibade et al., 2022) conducted a study using ensemble methods with various base learners, including k-NN, to predict student academic performance, affirming the performance improvement achieved through ensembling. Similarly, (Ajibade et al., 2019) propose a performance prediction model utilizing behavioral features of students, employing ensemble methods such as Bagging, Boosting, and Random Forest to enhance classifier performance.

(Mahfouz et al., 2021) propose an ensemble classifier, EKNN, for cancer diagnosis using microarray-based approaches, addressing challenges such as high dimensionality and sample imbalance. (Mehanovic et al., 2020) emphasize timely heart disease detection, exploring the effectiveness of ensemble learning techniques using artificial neural networks, k-nearest neighbor, and support vector machines. (Swarna et al., 2022) present an ensemble Random Subspace (RS) classifier for detecting faults in photovoltaic connected power networks.

(Zhang et al., 2019) introduce the Weighted Heterogeneous Distance Metric (WHDM) and a progressive kNN classifier, enhancing diversity through the Reduced Random Subspace-based Bagging (RRSB) algorithm. (Sinta et al., 2014) evaluate the performance of ensemble KNN methods, demonstrating improved accuracy compared to standalone KNN. (Xiao, 2019) proposes an ensemble learning approach for traffic incident detection, combining SVM and KNN models for enhanced performance and robustness.

(Grabowski, 2002) proposes an ensemble of k-NN classifiers, each trained on a random partition of the training set, while (Gul et al., 2018) propose ES-kNN, an ensemble of a subset of kNN classifiers, showcasing their potential in classification tasks.

1.10 Decision trees

The decision tree (Quinlan, 1986) serves as a data mining tool utilized to visually represent a set of choices in a tree format. It stands as one of the most widely used supervised learning methods for addressing data classification challenges. Essentially, a decision tree constructs a hierarchy of tests to make predictions. There exist two primary types of decision trees:

- **Regression Trees**: These are employed to forecast numerical values, such as predicting the price of a house or the number of goals scored in a football match.
- **Classification Trees**: These are used to predict the class to which the output variable belongs. For instance, they can effectively determine an animal's sex based on certain characteristics like color and form.

1.10.1 Learning phase

During the construction phase, the decision tree expands by adding new nodes to its structure. Each node plays the role of dividing the population of individuals into more homogeneous subgroups (as depicted in Figure 1.13). To accomplish this, each node is associated with a partitioning rule that guides the distribution of individuals into the appropriate subgroup.

The process of determining the partitioning rule at each node of a decision tree involves the following steps:

1. Selecting a Partitioning Attribute: For each node, one of the input variables corresponding to the individual's attributes is chosen as the partitioning criterion.
2. Defining Partitioning Tests: Based on the values of the chosen attribute within the node's population, one or more tests are defined to partition the individuals into subsets.

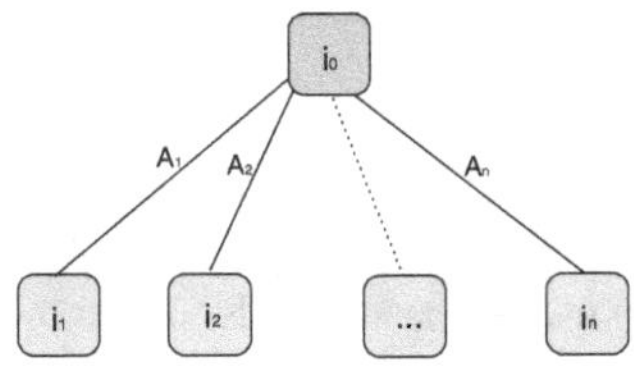

FIGURE 1.13 – Partition of a set of individuals within a decision tree. In this case, i_0 denotes the population of the root node, and i_1, i_2, ..., i_n represent the subsets resulting from this partition. The attributes $A_1, ..., A_n$ determine how individuals are distributed among the child nodes.

3. Distributing Individuals: Each individual is subjected to the partitioning tests and distributed into the appropriate subsets, resulting in the creation of new branches with as many new nodes as there are partitions.
4. Repeating the Process: The same process is repeated with all these new nodes until only leaf nodes are left at each branch's end. A leaf node is one that has no children and is considered sufficiently homogeneous to avoid further partitioning. A leaf is called "pure" if its population belongs to only one class.

The notion of purity or impurity often serves as the main criterion for stopping a tree's growth. If a leaf is pure, there is no need to continue partitioning its population. However, additional stop criteria may also be used to halt tree growth, especially when the tree becomes too complex. Pruning techniques can be applied to reduce the tree's size and complexity after it reaches its maximum size (Breiman et al., 1984; Quinlan, 1987; Mingers, 1989; Quinlan, 1993; Malerba et al., 1996; Esposito et al., 1997; Breslow and Aha, 1997; Sebbanü et al., 2000). Pruning involves removing unnecessary branches from the tree, and it is implemented in induction algorithms to enhance the generalization capabilities of decision trees. If no pruning is performed, a tree might over-learn the training data and perform poorly on generalization.

To improve the generalization capability, several decision trees can be combined. Ensemble classifiers take advantage of trees' instability by manipulating the training data for each tree. By building trees on different learning sets, their structures will differ, as they over-learn those sets. Consequently, pruning techniques are generally not used in decision tree ensembles. Random forest algorithms, for instance, do not employ pruning methods and let the tree induction continue until only pure leaves are obtained.

Finally, after building a tree, the last step is to assign a conclusion to each leaf. When no additional stop tests or pruning have been applied, and all leaves are pure, the conclusions for each leaf are straightforward. Typically, the prediction assigned to a not-pure leaf corresponds to the most represented class among the training data contained therein (Quinlan, 1987; Mingers, 1989; Esposito et al., 1997). Other techniques exist and are implemented when stop criteria or pruning procedures are used. However, when working with forests, such processes are not necessary, as the trees are induced up to their maximum size.

To summarize, the construction of a decision tree involves the following steps (starting from the root of the tree):

1. Select a partitioning attribute among the attributes that describe the training data.
2. Define one or more threshold values of this attribute to establish the partition.
3. Repeat steps 1 and 2 with each child node that does not meet the criteria to become leaves (if all child nodes are pure leaves, the current branch has reached its maximum depth).
4. Prune the tree if necessary.
5. Assign each leaf a conclusion.

While pruning and assigning decisions to the leaves are not crucial for inducing trees in random forests, the choice of the partitioning rule at each node plays an important role, particularly in understanding the challenges of using randomization principles for random forest induction. Therefore, more details will be provided on this step

1.10.2 Evaluation of partitioning rules

Most tree induction methods follow a common process for selecting partitioning attributes at each node. This involves evaluating various candidate characteristics by partitioning the data and then calculating a quality criterion for each partition. The attribute that optimizes this criterion is chosen for the node split. Consequently, the methods differ based on the evaluation criterion used to assess the quality of the splitting.

Selecting the appropriate criterion for partitioning rule selection has been a subject of extensive research since the introduction of the first tree induction algorithms by (Breiman et al., 1984) and (Quinlan, 1986). Numerous studies have addressed the topic of feature selection for partitioning, and Murthy's state-of-the-art on Induction of Decision Trees provides a comprehensive list of references on this matter (Murthy, 1998).

In 1989, (Mingers, 1989) listed and compared 11 main criteria used for evaluating partitioning rules in tree induction algorithms. Surprisingly, he found that random selection of a partitioning characteristic yielded effective results comparable to other criteria.

In 1992, Buntine and Niblett (bun) challenged the rigor of Mingers' experimental protocol and conducted their own empirical comparison of 4 out of the 11 measures. They found contrasting results, indicating that random attribute selection performed significantly worse than the other methods in their tests.

In most cases, the evaluation criterion for partitioning rules is based on a measure of impurity. Impurity refers to the impurity of a distribution of class labels in a population, measured through various methods. The impurity measure should be at its minimum when all individuals in a node belong to the same class and at its maximum when each class is equally represented in the node's population.

(Murthy, 1998) classifies three non-exclusive categories of criteria in his work: information theory-based criteria (e.g., Shannon's Entropy), distance-based criteria (e.g., the Gini index), and criteria based on dependencies (e.g., statistical measures of the $\chi 2$ test type).

In the subsequent paragraphs, we delve into the three main criteria used in the context of random forests. These criteria are employed in the ID3 (Quinlan, 1986), C4.5 (Quinlan, 1993), and CART (Breiman et al., 1984) decision tree induction algorithms, which are widely implemented in various machine learning software.

- **Information gain**
  Quinlan's tree induction algorithm, known as ID3 (Induction Decision Tree), utilizes the criterion of Information Gain (Quinlan, 1986). The concept of impurity can be evaluated in various ways, and for Information Gain, it involves quantifying the information required to determine the class of an individual within a population T. This is estimated using the Shannon Entropy formula, where the corresponding probabilities are inferred from observed frequencies.

$$I(T) = \sum_{j=1}^{c} \frac{n_{j.}}{n_{..}} \log_2 \frac{n_{j.}}{n_{..}} \tag{1.7}$$

  where $n_{j.}$ denotes number of data points belonging to class j, and the dot notation signifies summation over the corresponding index.

  Let's imagine that we have a scenario where the population T is divided into m_i sub-groups of individuals labeled as $T_1, T_2, ..., T_{m_i}$ based on the values of attribute A_i. Here, m_i represents the number of categories (modalities) for attribute A_i.

  In this context, the information required to determine the class of any individual in the entire population T can be represented as a weighted average of the information needed to determine the class of an individual within each sub-group T_k:

$$I(T, A_i) = \sum_{k=1}^{m_i} \frac{n_{.k}}{n_{..}} I(T_k) \tag{1.8}$$

$n_{.k}$ denotes the size of class k for sub-group T_k.
$n_{..}$ is the total size of the population (the sum of all sub-groups' sizes).
$I(T_k)$ represents the information (entropy) needed to identify the class of an element within sub-group T_k.

After calculating the impurity using the aforementioned equation, the resulting measure known as Information Gain, represented as Gain(T, A_i), is defined as follows:

$$Gain(T, A_i) = \Delta I(T, A_i) = I(T) - I(T, A_i) \tag{1.9}$$

where:
$I(T)$: It represents the impurity in the entire dataset T.
$I(T, A_i)$: It represents the impurity of the dataset T after it has been split based on attribute A_i.

- **Gain Ratio**
  A correction was later introduced to the Information Gain criterion to address its bias towards attributes with many categories. This corrected version is known as the Relative Information Gain or Gain Ratio.

$$IV(T, A_i) = -\sum_{k=1}^{m_i} \frac{n_{.k}}{n_{..}} \log_2 \frac{n_{.k}}{n_{..}} \tag{1.10}$$

$$GainRatio(T, A_i) = \frac{Gain(T, A_i)}{IV(T, A_i)} \tag{1.11}$$

  where the function $IV(A_i)$ calculates the intrinsic information of attribute A_i, while the Gain Ratio represents its Relative Information Gain.

- **Gini index**
  This criterion was introduced and employed by Breiman et al. in the Classification And Regression Tree (CART or C&RT) method (Breiman et al., 1984). It is also the criterion of choice adopted by Breiman in his algorithms for creating random forests. The following formula is used to measure the impurity of a population:

$$I(T) = \sum_{j=1}^{c} (\frac{n_{j.}}{n_{..}})^2 \tag{1.12}$$

  We also encounter this criterion in the literature (Breiman et al., 1984) in the following form:

$$I(T) = 1 - \sum_{j=1}^{c} \frac{n_{j.}}{n_{..}}(1 - \frac{n_{j.}}{n_{..}}) \tag{1.13}$$

  This measure can be interpreted as the expected classification error if the predicted class was chosen randomly based on the class probabilities estimated from the number of instances in the current node T. Similar to Information Gain, it facilitates the computation of the impurity gain resulting from partitioning with a specific attribute.

$$\Delta I(T, A_i) = I(T) - \sum_{k=1}^{m_i} \frac{n_{.k}}{n_{..}} I(T_k) \tag{1.14}$$

Similarly, by considering T_k as the population of the k-th child node, where k corresponds to the value of the attribute $A_i = k$.

The existing criteria for evaluating partitioning rules in decision trees do not significantly stand out from each other, as concluded by various studies (Hssina et al., 2014; Singh and Gupta, 2014). The differences observed in the resulting trees based on different criteria are not substantial enough to yield significant variations in the results. The crucial factor that influences the tree structures is not the evaluation criteria but rather the training data.

One of the main drawbacks of decision trees is their instability. These classifiers tend to overfit the training data, making them heavily reliant on how well the training data represent the problem domain. Even a minor change in the training set can lead to significant alterations in the tree structure, impacting its generalization capabilities.

This instability has driven researchers to focus on sets of decision trees. While it may be a clear weakness for an individual classifier, it can be turned into a strength when dealing with ensembles of classifiers, such as decision forests. By manipulating the training data and introducing substantial variations for each decision tree within the ensemble, diversity can be achieved. These differences in structures and predictions among the trees result in overall enhanced diversity.

In the following section, we provide a review of the research on sets of decision trees, illustrating how researchers have gradually defined and utilized what we now refer to as decision forests.

1.11 Ensemble of classifiers

The field of combining classifiers has a rich and extensive literature. The concept of forming a committee by combining multiple experts dates back to the mid-1960s (Nilsson, 1965), and since then, it has gained significant traction, especially in the 1990s. Nowadays, there is substantial research focused on formalizing, analyzing, understanding, and advancing this field.

Dedicated works solely devoted to this topic exist (Kuncheva, 2014), and annual workshops are specifically organized to explore various aspects of classifier combination (Kettler and Roli, 2000; Kittler and Roli, 2001; Roli and Kittler, 2002b; Windeatt and Roli, 2003; Roli and Kittler, 2004; Oza et al., 2005; Haindl et al., 2007; Benediktsson et al., 2009). Furthermore, international journals in the domain of machine learning and pattern recognition often publish special issues dedicated to this subject (Fairhurst et al., 1990; Roli and Kittler, 2002a; Dasarathy, 2005).

With the extensive research and interest in the field, there has been a harmonization of different taxonomies proposed to categorize the numerous related works. This harmonization facilitates better organization and understanding of the multitude of approaches explored in the area of classifier combination.

- **Statistical limitation (variance):**
  The statistical limitation arises when the search space for classifiers, induced by learning algorithms, becomes significantly large relative to the available data for learning. In such situations, multiple classifiers, equally efficient in learning, can be induced, leaving the learning algorithm to "choose" only one of them. However, this selection process may lead to the choice of a "bad" classifier that is not effective in generalization.

  To address this challenge, a potential solution is to combine the predictions of several classifiers that have demonstrated efficiency in learning. This ensemble of classifiers, denoted as h_c, proves to be much more beneficial than individual classifiers alone, as it better approximates the true function f. Figure 1.14 visually illustrates this situation, representing the space of possible classifiers H, within which a subset of best-performing classifiers in learning is depicted. The combining classifier (h_c) emerges as a more compelling option, significantly approaching the true function f compared to the set of individual classifiers it combines.

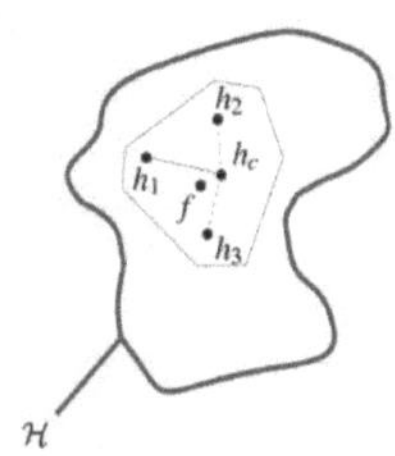

FIGURE 1.14 – Schematic illustration of the statistical limitation of unique classifiers.

- **Limitation of representation (bias):**
  In many machine learning scenarios, the true function f cannot be accurately represented by any single classifier within the search space H. To overcome this limitation, it is possible to extend the search space H by incorporating classifiers that combine multiple individual classifiers from the original space, as illustrated in Figure 1.15. By doing so, we can achieve a better approximation of the function f beyond the limitations of the original space H.

One example of this approach is seen in solving multi-class classification problems using learning algorithms designed for two-class problems. In such cases, when the goal is to address multi-class problems exclusively using binary classifiers (capable of handling two-class problems only), a common strategy is to solve the binary subproblems separately. The final decision is then made by combining the decisions from these intermediate binary subproblems. This approach is frequently adopted with Support Vector Machine (SVM) classifiers, as these methods initially support only two-class problems (Hsu and Lin, 2002). By combining binary classifiers, this technique enables tackling multi-class classification challenges more effectively.

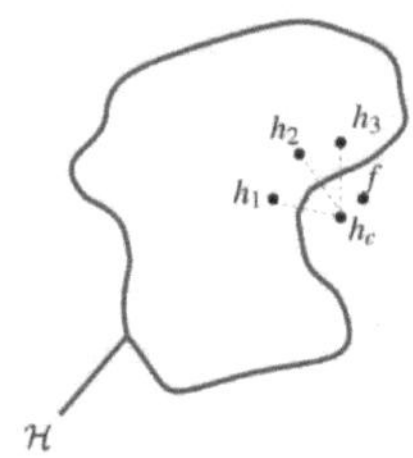

FIGURE 1.15 – Schematic illustration of the representation limitation of unique classifiers.

- **Computational limitation:**
  The third and final limitation in classifier learning is computational in nature. Many learning algorithms employ local heuristic search within the space H, which may lead to the selection of a locally optimal classifier that is suboptimal globally. In simpler terms, the chosen classifier may appear to approach the true function f based on the algorithm's search criteria but is, in reality, only an intermediate solution. Dietterich provides an example in his article (Dietterich, 2000a), citing neural networks that often use gradient descent to minimize learning error, and decision trees that partition the description space recursively and not exhaustively.

  The challenge arises from the fact that a training algorithm's broad search to avoid local optima can be computationally expensive. Nevertheless, in such situations, it is possible to mitigate the risk of choosing a suboptimal classifier by combining several of the suboptimal (locally optimal) classifiers, as demonstrated in Figure 1.16. By obtaining a set of classifiers derived from running multiple heuristic searches from different points in the space H, a better approximation of f can be achieved. This ensemble of classifiers provides a more robust and improved solution compared to relying on a single locally optimal classifier.

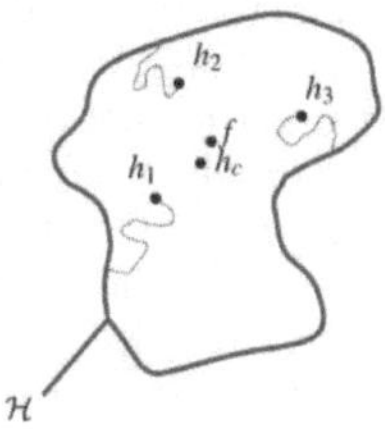

FIGURE 1.16 – Schematic illustration of the computational limitation of unique classifiers.

Dietterich highlights three fundamental limitations leading to the failure of single classifier algorithms. EoCs (Ensemble of Classifiers) offer an appealing solution to these challenges. While rooted in statistical learning theory, more practical reasons exist for combining classifiers instead of using single ones. One immediate reason is the gain in precision achieved by aggregating the outputs of multiple classifiers for a more reliable decision. This addresses one of Dietterich's mentioned limitations as it allows compensating for errors with the majority of accurate predictions from other classifiers. Another reason for combining classifiers is the complexity of the problem at hand. When a single classifier struggles to handle the complexity, breaking it down into simpler subproblems and solving them separately with different classifiers can be effective. Decision-making then involves combining these classifiers' results.

The famous "no free lunch theorem" in digital optimization applies to machine learning, showing that no unique model or classifier can solve all types of problems (Wolpert and Macready, 1997). As a result, it becomes more relevant to work at a higher level of problem-solving. Managerial systems can leverage multiple lower-level solving systems, such as combinations of classifiers, to make the most of their collective capabilities (Minsky, 1991). In conclusion, there are several reasons why one might consider combining multiple classifiers:

- Enhanced Reliability: By incorporating advice from several experts instead of just one, decisions become more reliable.
- Increased Complexity: Combining classifiers provides more complex models, surpassing what single classifiers can achieve.
- Avoidance of Local Optima: The ensemble approach helps avoid getting stuck in local optima during the learning process.
- Handling Complexity: It enables handling extremely complex problems that cannot be fully understood as a whole.
- Greater Generality: Ensemble classifiers offer a more generic and effective approach for solving a wide range of problems.

These advantages stem from an essential characteristic of multiclassifier systems known as "diversity." The concept of diversity is widely accepted

within the community, as it accounts for each of these benefits in contrast to unique classifiers (Kuncheva and Whitaker, 2003; Kuncheva, 2003, 2014).
If there is no universally agreed-upon formal definition of diversity in the scientific community, it can be intuitively understood as the differences between elementary classifiers within a set. To achieve a performance gain, a set of classifiers must exhibit reasonable differences from one another. Diversity is quantified in machine learning to capture these differences. In the context of classification, diversity refers to the ability of an ensemble of classifiers to agree on good predictions and disagree on prediction errors. The challenge in combining classifiers often lies in generating diversity among the elementary classifiers in the ensemble (Kuncheva et al., 2000; Banfield et al., 2003; Kuncheva, 2003, 2014; Brown et al., 2005). Various approaches exist to achieve this. In the next section, we will discuss the different paradigms of combining classifiers and the diverse approaches to constructing multi-classifier systems.

1.11.1 Principles of induction of an ensemble of classifiers

1.11.1.1 Bagging

In its "classic" version, Bagging is categorized as a data manipulation method in the taxonomy of the principles of induction of Ensemble of Classifiers (EoCs). It applies the principle of Bootstrap, or Bootstrapping, to aggregate classifiers, which is why it is called Bagging, short for Bootstrap Aggregating.

Bootstrap is a statistical resampling principle (Efron and Tibshirani, 1994) commonly used for estimating quantities or statistical properties. Bootstrap not only improves the reliability of statistical estimates but also provides additional information on these estimates. It enables the calculation of dispersion (e.g., standard deviation or variance) of measurements, confidence intervals, and tests of hypotheses. In statistics, when approximating the distribution of a population of data, an empirical distribution of observed data is typically used. The bootstrap approach goes beyond using a single empirical distribution by creating multiple sets of data resampled from all the observed data, using random selection with replacement. Let's assume we have a set $T = x_1, x_2, x_3, ..., x_N$ of N observed data points from our population, and we are interested in a statistic denoted as $S(T)$. The bootstrap process involves forming L samples $T_k^* = (x'_1 x'_2 x'_3 ..., x'_{N'})$ for $k = 1, ..., L$, where each T_k^* is created by randomly drawing N' data points from T with replacement (as illustrated in Figure 1.17). These L samples are commonly referred to as the bootstrap samples. Subsequently, we calculate $S(T_k^*)$ for each bootstrap sample, resulting in L estimates of the statistic. This approach offers an empirical distribution of our statistics instead of a single estimate from one run. By computing the empirical mean from these values (cf. Equation 1.15), we derive a more precise estimate of the statistic. Alternatively, we can assess its dispersion by computing the standard error (cf. Equation 1.16). Employing bootstrap resampling enables us to gain insights into the

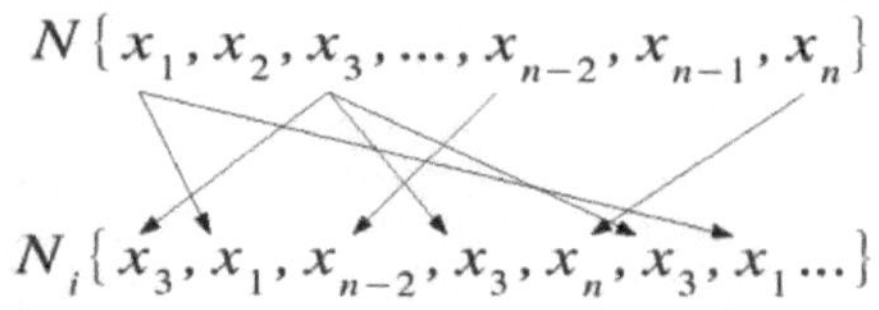

FIGURE 1.17 – Illustration of a random draw with replacement for the formation of a bootstrap sample.

variability of the statistic and provides a robust framework for estimating its properties based on multiple resampled datasets.

$$S_{boot} = \sum_{k=1}^{L} \frac{S(T_k^*)}{L} \tag{1.15}$$

$$\hat{se}_{boot} = \sqrt{\frac{\sum_{k=1}^{L} (S(T_k^*) - S_{boot})^2}{L-1}} \tag{1.16}$$

Based on the principle of resampling(Breiman, 1996) Breiman introduced n 1996 the Bagging method. This method involves considering the statistic of interest as a learning algorithm denoted as $h(x)$ and applying the bootstrap principle as previously explained. Each elementary classifier $h_k(x)$ in the ensemble is trained on one of the L bootstrap samples, resulting in different training sets. Figure 1.18 illustrates the Bagging process applied to an ensemble of decision trees. Breiman's principle of "meta-learning" is ap-

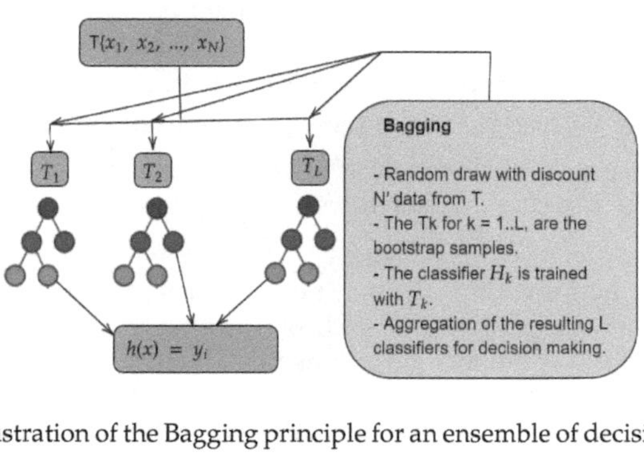

FIGURE 1.18 – Illustration of the Bagging principle for an ensemble of decision trees.

plicable to all types of learning algorithms, but he primarily experimented with decision trees (Breiman, 1996). The reason behind this choice is that Bagging's main strength lies in reducing the instability of a classifier. Instability in this context refers to the fact that a small change in the learning data can lead to significant variations in the tree's structure and, consequently, its performance during generalization. By reducing this instability, Bagging enhances the reliability of predictions and improves overall generalization performance. However, decision trees are inherently very unstable classifiers, making them an ideal candidate for Bagging experiments. Breiman extensively discusses the effects of bagging on the instability of a classifier, leading to the conclusion that the classifier's instability plays a crucial role in the effectiveness of bagging for classification tasks. When bagging an unstable classifier, it tends to improve the average generalization error. However, bagging a stable classifier is not as effective in reducing the error (Breiman, 1996; Skurichina, 2001; Grandvalet, 2004).

Skurichina's work in (Skurichina, 2001) delves into the issue of classifier stability and conducts extensive experiments using Bagging to reduce the instability of various classifiers. The results show that Bagging does not enhance the performance of stable classifiers, such as k-Plus Near Neighbors, as it does for unstable ones. This observation underlines the significance of the classifier's stability in determining the impact of bagging on generalization performance.

1.11.1.2 Random Subspaces

The Random Subspace technique, often abbreviated as RSM, shares a conceptual similarity with Bagging (Ho, 1995, 1998; Bryll et al., 2003). Unlike focusing on the training data, this approach operates on the attributes themselves. The fundamental idea involves training individual classifiers within randomly selected subspaces of the feature space. These subspaces, each with a dimension of P, where P is less than the overall dimension M of the original feature space, are employed for the induction of elementary classifier h_k.This induction process involves the following steps:

1. Randomly selecting P features from the pool of M available features without replacement.
2. Projecting all training data into this newly formed subspace of features.
3. Training the classifier h_k on these projections of the training data.

Figure 1.19 visually demonstrates the implementation of this procedure in the context of inducing decision forests.

In the work by (Ho, 1998), it is demonstrated that optimal outcomes are achieved when the parameter P is chosen around $P \approx M/2$, as highlighted in her research. Additionally, Ho illustrates that this technique proves especially effective when the description space contains a specific level of redundant information distributed across all characteristics, rather than being concentrated within a subset. It's noteworthy that the RSM can be applied to various types of elementary classifiers. In numerous studies, it has been employed for building ensembles of decision trees (Ho, 1992, 1995; Banfield et al., 2006; Latinne et al., 2000, 2002). This approach holds an advantage over other methods for generating decision forests, mainly due to its ability to reduce the dimensionality of the training data's description space.

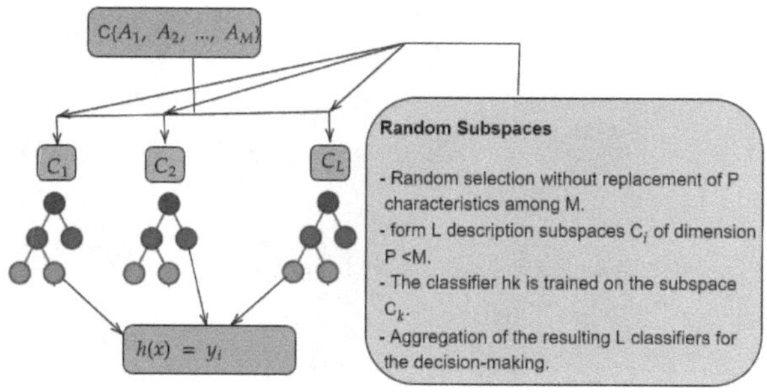

FIGURE 1.19 – Illustration of the principle of Random Subspaces for an ensemble of decision trees.

While the automatic induction of decision trees typically requires multiple passes through this space, utilizing the RSM substantially decreases the computational cost compared to alternative decision forest induction techniques that do not alter the decision tree induction algorithm. Beyond computational considerations, the reduction in the description space's size, while keeping the volume of training data constant, plays a pivotal role in explaining the effectiveness of the RSM approach. By diminishing this space's dimensions, the method maintains stability even with a reduced number of training instances, mitigating the instability and high variance often associated with classifiers trained on datasets where the number of features exceeds the training instances, often referred to as the "curse of dimensionality."

Moreover, in cases where the description space features substantial information redundancy, training a classifier on a subset of characteristics can be more efficient than using the entire set. Combining classifiers of this nature frequently enhances performance beyond what a single classifier could achieve, thereby contributing to stable classifiers.

1.11.1.3 Boosting

Boosting is an ensemble technique in machine learning that aims to enhance the predictive capabilities of weaker models by combining them into a more powerful collective predictor. Figure 1.20 schematizes the architecture of this combination of classifiers. The core concept of boosting involves training a series of weaker models in a step-by-step manner, with each subsequent model focusing on correcting the errors made by its predecessors.

Here's a breakdown of the boosting process:

1. **Initialization**: Initially, all training instances are assigned equal weights, representing their significance in the learning process.
2. **Sequential Training**: A weak learner, often a simple model like a decision tree stump, is trained using the data. Special emphasis is placed

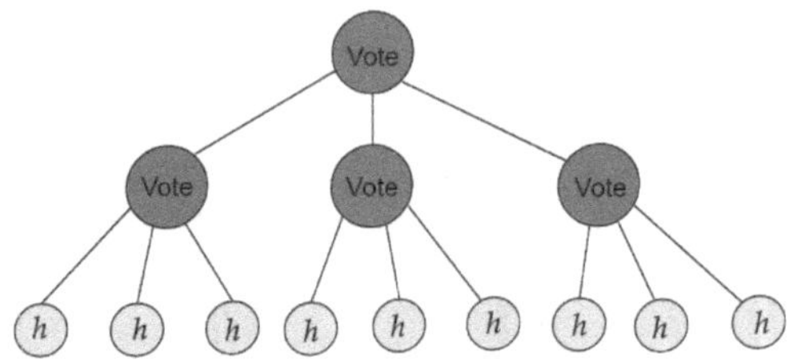

FIGURE 1.20 – Illustration of the first boosting algorithm proposed by Schapire in (Schapire, 1990). Each "h" node is a weak classifier, and each "Vote" node is a plurality voting operator.

on instances that were incorrectly predicted by earlier models. The aim of this weak learner is to rectify the mistakes made by previous models.

3. **Weighted Combination**: After training, the error of the weak learner is calculated, and instance weights are adjusted. Instances that the latest model misclassified are given higher weights, whereas correctly classified instances receive lower weights.
4. **Iterative Process**: Steps 2 and 3 are repeated for a set number of iterations or until a specific stopping point is reached. During each iteration, a new weak learner is trained on the adjusted data, and the ensemble is updated accordingly.
5. **Final Prediction**: The ultimate prediction is generated by amalgamating the predictions from all weak learners. The predictions are weighted based on the performance of their respective models during training.

Boosting techniques like AdaBoost and Gradient Boosting have demonstrated their effectiveness by significantly enhancing the performance of weak models. They have achieved remarkable results across diverse machine-learning tasks, encompassing both classification and regression. Unlike bagging methods that prioritize variance reduction through diverse model creation, boosting is geared toward bias reduction by progressively refining model accuracy.

1.11.2 From the tree to the forest

The initial algorithms for constructing decision trees used in classification were introduced during the 1980s. The CHAID algorithm emerged in this period, focusing on Chi-square AID (Kass, 1980). The exploration of automated decision tree generation gained momentum during this era. Breiman and Quinlan played pivotal roles in 1984 and 1986 by presenting their respective CART algorithms (Breiman et al., 1984) and ID3 algorithm (Quinlan, 1986). Quinlan expanded on ID3's principles in 1993 with the C4.5 algorithm

(Quinlan, 1993), which, along with CART, is now considered a cornerstone for automated decision tree induction. Concurrently, in the early 1990s, research emerged on amalgamating decision trees. In 1990, (Shlien, 1990) proposed employing combined decision trees for handwritten character recognition, utilizing Dempster-Shafer theory to establish consensus among trees. Dietterich introduced the Error-Correcting Output Codes (ECOC) method in 1991 (Dietterich and Bakiri, 1991), a framework for learning classifier sets, which he initially experimented with using decision trees. He demonstrated ECOC's efficacy in enhancing performance for multi-class problems with binary classifiers. In 1992, (Ho, 1992) highlighted the performance improvement achievable by parallel combinations of classifiers employing multiple decision trees. In 1995, (Ho and decision Forest, 1995) introduced the term "Decision Forest" for sets of decision trees while also laying the groundwork for Random subspace methods.

These early efforts with randomized tree sets paved the way for subsequent randomization principles in the realm of decision forests. Notably, in 1996, Breiman introduced the Bagging principle (Breiman, 1996), a method for combining classifiers, showcasing its efficiency primarily in the context of decision trees. The same year, (Freund et al., 1996) unveiled the Boosting Adaboost algorithm, long regarded as an effective approach for learning sets of classifiers. Research on Boosting and Adaboost proliferated, expanding the literature on boosted tree sets. Amit and Geman introduced the Random Feature Selection principle in 1996 (Amit and Geman, 1997), a decision tree randomization concept. In 1998, (Ho, 1998) elaborated on Random Subspaces methods, illustrating their superiority over Bagging and Boosting in high-dimensional problems. Dietterich presented the Random Split Selection principle (Dietterich, 2000b) in the same year, akin to Amit and Geman's approach, showing that Adaboost remains the most efficient learning principle for decision forests in low-noise data scenarios.

Following the introduction of these induction principles for decision forests, various experimental studies compared and assessed their strengths and limitations. For instance, (Amit and Blanchard, 2001) examined and analyzed seven tree induction principles, introducing the acronym MRCL (Multiple Randomized Classifiers) to broadly denote principles of randomization for ensemble classifier induction. (Bauer and Kohavi, 1999) extensively studied the Bagging and Boosting methods' families, comparing different variants of these reference algorithms. Their empirical analyses shed light on the performance enhancements achievable with each family, with Boosting proving notably superior to Bagging in the context of decision trees.

It's important to note that these decision tree induction principles were established prior to Breiman's influential article, which introduced the term "Random Forest" and its associated formalism. Breiman's contribution was to provide a structured framework for this approach rather than inventing random forests outright. The following section delves into this framework, presenting the general definition of random forest methods and elaborating on their operational mechanisms.

1.12 Definition of random forest

At this point, we have already introduced a substantial portion of the foundational principles that underpin random forest methods. However, for a more intricate comprehension, it becomes imperative to expound upon the formal structure that intricately defines them; this elucidation forms the crux of the current section.

For a comprehensive grasp of random forests, it proves enlightening to begin by presenting the definition as put forth by Leo Breiman in his publication of 2001 within the esteemed Machine Learning journal (Breiman, 2001). The following is a direct rendition of this definition:

Definition 1. A Random Forest denotes a classifier comprised of a collection of elementary classifiers, all of which are of the decision tree category, and can be denoted as: $f(x, V_i),\ i = 1, ..., M$

Where V_i represents a set of independent and identically distributed random vectors, with each individual tree contributing to the collective decision regarding the most prevalent class for a given input data point x.

These succinct lines encapsulate the fundamental components that characterize random forests:

1. Random forests derive from collections of decision trees.
2. The induction process incorporates a degree of randomization.

The fundamental principles underpinning the creation of random forests are shaped by these two core concepts. In practical terms, it's evident that the avenues for constructing random forests are diverse, given that this definition doesn't impose restrictions on the specific randomness employed during tree induction. Nonetheless, there are a couple of additional points that warrant consideration as they are either implicitly implied or associated with this declaration:

(i) The first point revolves around the combination operator: the definition appears to endorse a majority voting approach—where each tree contributes to selecting the most prevalent class for an input data point, x. However, practical implementations have expanded this definition to encompass alternative combination operators. This broader spectrum of operators enables better tailoring to particular intricacies of distinct problems (Tsymbal et al., 2006; Breitenbach et al., 2003; Robnik-Šikonja, 2004).

(ii) The second aspect pertains to the formalization of randomization within the induction of random forest algorithms. This formalization involves introducing a random vector into the definition of elementary classifiers, denoted as $f(x, V_i)$. The ensemble of V_i thus constitutes a collection of random vectors that are independent and identically distributed. In practice, this signifies that when inducing random forests, each tree is developed autonomously, irrespective of the other decision trees already integrated into the forest (implying independence). Moreover, the randomization principle employed must be consistent across all trees in the forest (indicating identical distribution). The foundational theoretical results, notably advanced by Breiman, such as convergence (Breiman, 2001) and forest consistency (Breiman, 2004), heavily rest upon the assumptions of independence and uniform distribution. As far as our knowledge extends, no random forest induction algorithm operates outside this framework. These two tenets are critical, as Breiman then constructs theoretical outcomes based on these hypotheses for this class of algorithms. This encompasses the demonstration of the convergence of generalization errors as the number of trees within a forest increases. Additionally, it establishes an upper limit for this generalization error and introduces crucial concepts like strength and correlation. These properties play a pivotal role in comprehending the mechanisms underlying forest behavior, which is why we delve deeper into them in the subsequent section.

1.13 Validation techniques

Validation techniques in machine learning (ML) refer to the methods and processes used to evaluate the performance and generalization capabilities of a trained model on unseen data. The primary purpose of validation techniques is to ensure that the model's performance is not only good on the data it was trained on (training data) but also on new, unseen data (validation or test data). This helps to gauge the model's ability to generalize and make accurate predictions on real-world data.

The primary aim of validation techniques is to prevent overfitting, a situation where a model becomes too closely aligned with the training data and picks up on noise or random variations. Overfitting results in poor performance on new data since the model has essentially memorized the training samples instead of understanding significant patterns.

1.13.1 The train/test/validation split

The process involves dividing the available datasets into a Train/Test split and a validation set. This division step is pivotal in the field of machine learning owing to the fact that training the model on the complete dataset increases the risk of overfitting to the training set. This outcome diminishes the model's generalizability and produces results that are biased and unreliable. To formulate a machine learning model, it's customary to partition the data into three subsets: training, validation, and test. The training set is used to train the model, the validation set is used for model selection, and the test set is set aside for the final model evaluation. A typical data split involves allocating 60% of the data for training, 20% for validation, and 20% for testing. Properly creating the training, development (dev), and test sets is crucial for ensuring productivity. It's important that the dev and test sets are derived from the same distribution and are randomly selected from the entire dataset.

1.13.2 Holdout technique

The objective of holdout evaluation lies in assessing a model's performance on data distinct from its training data, thereby potentially offering an impartial estimation of a classifier's effectiveness. In this approach, the dataset is randomly divided into the following segments:

- Training set: This subset of the dataset is intended to facilitate model training.
- Validation set: It serves the purpose of evaluating the performance of the trained model, parameter-tuning, and making model selections.
- Test set: Reserved for the final evaluation phase.

The holdout technique is valued for its rapidity, straightforwardness, and adaptability. Nonetheless, this technique often comes with a drawback of high variability. Differences between the training and test datasets can lead to significant fluctuations in the performance estimate, particularly if the data distribution in the training set greatly differs from that in the validation/test sets.

1.13.3 Cross validation

Cross-validation stands as a widely recognized validation approach that involves splitting the entire dataset into training and testing sets. The testing set, unseen by the classifier during training, is employed to assess the model's performance. Various forms of cross-validation have been proposed within the literature, with k-fold cross-validation being the most prevalent.

K-fold cross-validation divides the complete dataset into approximately equal-sized subsets, where k-1 of these subsets are amalgamated into a training subset, leaving one subset aside for the ultimate model evaluation. This evaluation process is reiterated k times for different subsets, yielding a collection of k-trained models. The overall cross-validation performance is subsequently derived by calculating the mean average of the performance estimates from each model.

The cross-validation mechanism is illustrated in Figure 1.21, considering a scenario where k = 5.

StratifiedKFold represents a distinct iteration of the cross-validation method and emerges as a superb choice when addressing imbalanced datasets. This technique showcases its strength by dividing the entirety of the dataset into subsets, each carefully constructed to preserve an almost equal distribution across different classes. This approach proves highly advantageous in scenarios where class imbalances exist, enhancing the accuracy of performance evaluation across various class categories.

1.13.4 Statistical tests

Upon executing a specific machine learning algorithm multiple times, varying outcomes are produced—a scenario often encountered, as seen in processes like k-fold cross-validation. In such instances, statistical assessments

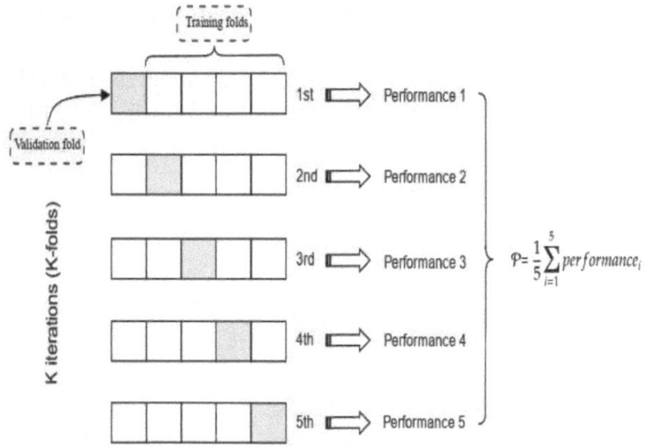

FIGURE 1.21 – K-folds cross-validation evaluation method with 5 folds.

can be conducted to ascertain whether noteworthy disparities exist among the medians associated with each technique. Within this book, the primary statistical approach employed is centered on the concept of standard deviation, which serves to quantify the extent of data dispersion. A diminished standard deviation signifies that the majority of outcomes are proximate to the mean (average). Conversely, an elevated standard deviation implies a broader distribution of values spanning a wider spectrum. Employing this measure can effectively illustrate the degree of variability across all iterations, thus providing insight into the dispersion of attained outcomes.

1.14 Evaluation metrics

1.14.1 Classification metrics

Classification quality measures serve as a yardstick to assess the reliability of outcomes derived from learned models. They furnish an objective basis for comparing multiple models.

In the context of classification, the foundation for evaluation lies within the realm of the confusion matrix. This matrix encapsulates essential elements forming the bedrock of evaluation metrics. It constitutes a table that juxtaposes predicted classes against observed classes. the fundamental elements of the confusion matrix are:

- True Positive (TP): Represents accurately predicted instances of positive events.
- True Negative (TN): Signifies accurately predicted instances of negative events.
- False Positive (FP): Denotes instances where positive events were incorrectly predicted.

- False Negative (FN): Signifies instances where negative events were incorrectly predicted.

By employing the confusion matrix (Figure 1.22), a range of established evaluation metrics can be formulated and computed for the assessment of binary classification.

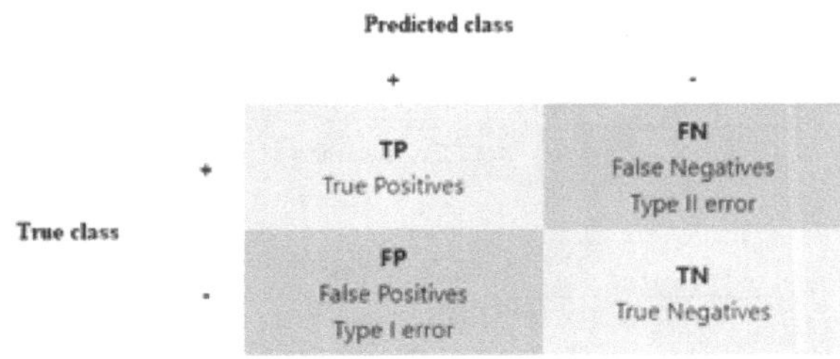

FIGURE 1.22 – The confusion matrix

Accuracy measures the proportion of correctly classified examples out of all examples. It is the most widely used metric for assessing the effectiveness of classifiers. The formula for calculating accuracy is:

$$Accuracy = \frac{TP + TN}{TP + TN + FP + FN} \tag{1.17}$$

Precision (PRE): measures the number of correct positive predictions. Therefore, the precision of the minority class determines its accuracy.

$$Precision = \frac{TP}{TP + FP} \tag{1.18}$$

Recall (REC): measures the percentage of actual positive instances correctly identified by the model. It indicates how well the model captures the positive class.

$$Recall = \frac{TP}{TP + FN} \tag{1.19}$$

F1-score (F1): is a metric that combines precision and recall, accounting for both false negative and false positive predictions. It is calculated using the following formula:

$$F1 - score = \frac{2 \times (Precision \times Recall)}{(Precision + Recall)} \tag{1.20}$$

The area under the roc curve (AUC) quantifies how well the positive cases are ranked above the negative cases and provides a comprehensive summary of model performance across all thresholds. It represents the probability that the model will rank a randomly chosen positive example higher than a randomly chosen negative example. Figure 1.23 illustrates the ROC curve, where the true positive rate (TPR) is plotted on the y-axis against the false positive rate (FPR) on the x-axis.

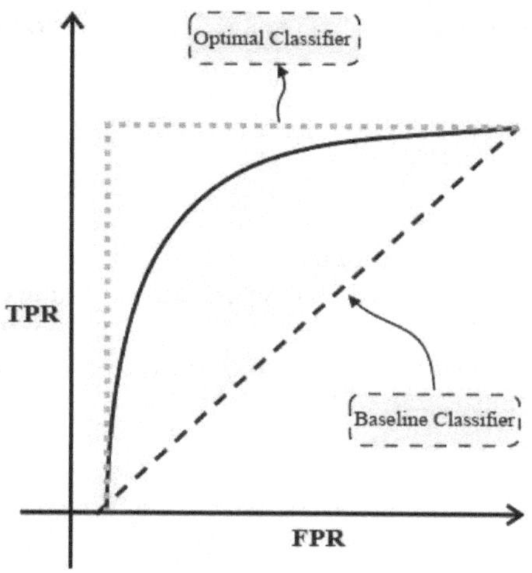

FIGURE 1.23 – ROC-AUC Curve: It quantifies the degree of separability. A higher AUC indicates a more effective classifier in distinguishing and classifying data examples.

Log loss (LOG) quantifies how well a classification model predicts probabilities, increasing as predictions diverge from actual labels. It is computed using the following formula:

$$logLoss = \frac{-1}{N}\sum_{i=1}^{N} y_i \times log(p_i) + (1 - p_i) \times log(1 - p_i) \quad (1.21)$$

Where "N" denotes the total number of instances, y_i represents the actual value of the label y, and p_i signifies the probability that y belongs to the positive class.

1.14.2 Clustering metrics

Evaluating the effectiveness of clustering algorithms is crucial for extracting meaningful insights from unlabeled data. A variety of performance metrics are available to assess the quality of clustering solutions. Below are several frequently employed performance metrics for the evaluation of clustering algorithms:

Calinski-Harabasz index

It also known as the Variance Ratio Criterion is another metric used to evaluate the quality of clustering results. It measures the ratio of between-cluster variance to within-cluster variance, essentially assessing the compactness and separation of clusters. Higher values of the Calinski-Harabasz Index indicate better clustering.

The formula for calculating the Calinski-Harabasz Index is as follows:

$$CH = \frac{B(k)}{W(k)} \times \frac{N-k}{k-1} \tag{1.22}$$

Where:

- k is the number of clusters.
- N is the total number of data points.
- $B(k)$ is the between-cluster variance, which quantifies the dispersion between cluster centroids.
- $W(k)$ is the within-cluster variance, which measures the average dispersion of data points within each cluster.

The formulas for $B(k)$ and $W(k)$ are:

$$W(k) = \sum_{i=1}^{k} \sum_{x \in C_i} \|x - c_i\|^2 \tag{1.23}$$

$$B_k = \sum_{i=1}^{k} n_i \times \|(c_i - c)\|^2 \tag{1.24}$$

Where:

- n_i is the number of data points in cluster i.
- c_i is the centroid of cluster i.
- c is the overall centroid of all data points.

Davies-Bouldin index

It is a metric used to evaluate the quality of clustering results. It measures the average similarity between each cluster and its most similar cluster, while also taking into account the distance between their centroids. Lower values of the Davies-Bouldin Index indicate better clustering.

The formula for calculating the Davies-Bouldin Index for a set of n clusters is as follows:

$$DB = \frac{1}{n} \sum_{i=1}^{n} \max_{j \neq i} \left\{ \frac{\sigma_i + \sigma_j}{d(c_i, c_j)} \right\} \tag{1.25}$$

Where:

- n is the number of clusters.

- σ_i is the average distance of all points in cluster i to the centroid c_i of cluster i.
- σ_j is the average distance of all points in cluster j to the centroid c_j of cluster j.
- $d(c_i, c_j)$ is the distance between the centroids c_i and c_j of clusters i and j, usually calculated using some distance metric (e.g., Euclidean distance).

The Silhouette Width Criterion

It is a metric used to evaluate the quality of clustering results by assessing how well-separated the clusters are and how similar each data point is to its own cluster compared to other clusters. It produces a score for each data point, and the average silhouette width across all data points gives an overall indication of the quality of the clustering.

The silhouette width $s(i)$ for a data point i is calculated using the following formula:

$$s(i) = \frac{1}{N}\frac{b_i - a_i}{max(a_i, b_i)} \tag{1.26}$$

Where

- $a(i)$ is the average distance from data point i to other points within the same cluster.
- $b(i)$ is the smallest average distance from data point i to points in a different cluster, representing its proximity to the nearest neighboring cluster

The silhouette width $s(i)$ ranges from -1 to 1:

- A high value of $s(i)$ indicates that the data point is well-matched to its own cluster and poorly matched to neighboring clusters.
- A value of $s(i)$ near 0 indicates that the data point is on or very close to the decision boundary between two neighboring clusters.
- A negative value of $s(i)$ indicates that the data point might have been assigned to the wrong cluster.

The average silhouette width of all data points, S, is then calculated to provide an overall evaluation of the clustering:

$$S = \frac{1}{N}\sum_{i=1}^{N} s(i) \tag{1.27}$$

Where N is the total number of data points.

1.15 Summary of the Chapter

In this chapter, we have presented essential definitions and concepts that are indispensable for delving into the intricacies of machine learning. These foundational ideas are crucial for a comprehensive understanding of the core book underpinning our research topic. Our primary focus has been on exploring various facets, encompassing data types, different learning paradigms, classification, regression tasks, and providing insights into decision trees, K-Nearest Neighbors (KNN), Association rules, clustering, and Random Forest.

In the upcoming Chapter 2, we will delve into the state-of-the-art methods, offering critical analyses and comparisons of each algorithm, including their respective advantages and disadvantages. Additionally, we will provide pseudo-code for the most widely used methods and conduct empirical comparisons to evaluate their performance and applicability.

Chapter 2

Modified decision trees

Contents

This section presents two modified decision tree algorithms. The initial algorithm introduces a novel pre-pruning technique, while the subsequent one enhances weak nodes by supplementing their data with that from comparable nodes.

In the first finding, we treat the problem of overfitting in the decision tree algorithm, pre-pruning emerges as a vital strategy to prevent excessive complexity and the risk of overfitting the training data. Rather than permitting the tree to continue growing until it precisely matches the training data, pre-pruning introduces specific conditions and limitations during the tree-building phase. Despite the existence of various pruning techniques today, achieving an optimal balance between structural simplicity and classification accuracy remains an ongoing challenge. As a response, we introduce a novel pre-pruning approach grounded in node-probability to address this issue.

The second finding tackles the issue of weak nodes in a distinct manner from the methods delineated in section (2.4). We introduce a novel algorithm labeled as EWNDT (Enhancing Weak Nodes in Decision Tree), which enhances weak nodes by incorporating additional data from similar nodes within the tree structure. This process is termed "data virtual merging," since it is temporary and is employed for recalculating the optimal split attribute and threshold within the weak node. We adopt two methodologies to ascertain the similarity between nodes. Comparative evaluations are performed with four leading decision tree techniques, and outcomes across 20 databases sourced from the UCI Repository underscore the superior performance of the EWNDT algorithm.

2.1 A new decision tree pre-pruning method based on nodes probabilities

2.1.1 Introduction

In many cases, decision trees can inadvertently fit the noise present in the training data, especially when some training samples are misclassified. This form of overfitting, where the tree becomes excessively tailored to the training data, can lead to suboptimal performance when applied to unseen examples, especially if the training data contains errors (Breiman et al., 1984). To mitigate this issue, the original tree can undergo a process known as pruning. Pruning involves the removal of certain components of the tree that hinder its ability to classify unseen examples effectively. This results in a simplified and more interpretable tree structure.

This technique of pruning can be applied to the construction of a decision tree classifier in two different ways:

- Stop the subdivision of the training data during the tree's construction (pre-pruning).
- Remove some parts of the tree structure by recursive after the construction of the tree is completed (post-pruning).

Therefore,We introduce a novel pre-pruning method that integrates two criteria: the size of the data within a node and the node's probability. The rationale behind the first criterion is that nodes with too few examples yield low-quality branches upon further partitioning. The second criterion is chosen because a node with a probability exceeding a certain threshold indicates near purity, making additional splits unnecessary.

2.1.2 Motivation

Using strict stopping criteria during the growth phase of a decision tree results in compact, underfit trees, while loose stopping criteria lead to overly complex, overfit trees. The most commonly employed stopping criteria include:

- **Maximum Depth**: Stops the creation of child nodes once the tree reaches a specified depth during initial construction.
- **Minimum Split Size**: Halts further splitting of a node when the number of observations falls below a specified minimum.
- **Minimum Leaf Size**: Discontinues node splitting when one of the child nodes has fewer observations than the defined minimum leaf size.

In the tree construction process, relying solely on the maximum tree depth criterion can result in imbalanced splits. For example, a leaf with 25,000 observations may stop splitting due to the depth limit, while another leaf with only 30 observations may continue to split. This imbalance seems counterintuitive since the splitting of nodes should be based on statistical rationale. For instance, partitioning a node with 100 observations into two child nodes one with 90 observations and the other with 10 lacks clear justification.

By refining the stopping rules, we aim to reduce the tree's size and prevent overfitting. This process, known as pre-pruning, aims to decrease the number of levels in the tree while avoiding the creation of nodes with insufficient examples. In other words, the goal is to strike a balance between tree complexity and classification performance.

2.1.3 Developed approach

In this research paper, we introduce an innovative stopping criterion designed to address the limitations of previous methods. Our approach involves terminating the construction of a decision tree when two specific conditions are met:

When the number of samples in a node falls below a predefined threshold, denoted as α (e.g., $\alpha = 10$).

When the probability of the majority class within that node exceeds a designated threshold, denoted as β (e.g., $\beta = 0.9$).

To illustrate this, let's consider the Titanic dataset. Figure 2.1 displays a part of the decision tree generated from this dataset. We have chosen $\alpha = 10$ as the minimum node size threshold, indicating a node's vulnerability, and $\beta = 0.8$ as the probability threshold, specifying the required probability for the majority class.

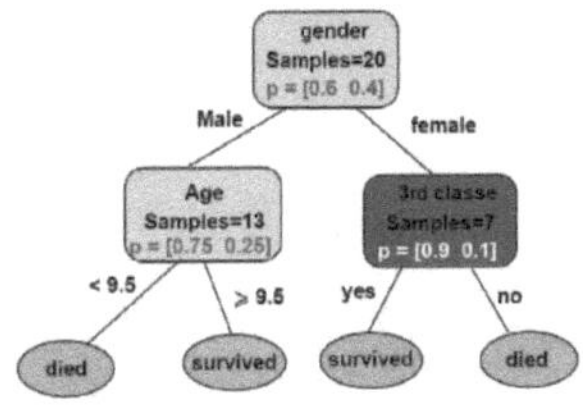

FIGURE 2.1 – Example of part of a decision tree created using the Titanic dataset

By applying our method to the tree depicted in Figure 2.1, we identify the node highlighted in red as weak and consequently subject it to pruning. Subsequently, it is replaced by a leaf node, as illustrated in Figure 2.2. Our algorithm meticulously assesses the validity of node splits, permitting a split only when the number of examples is substantial, and the probability of class membership is not exceedingly high.

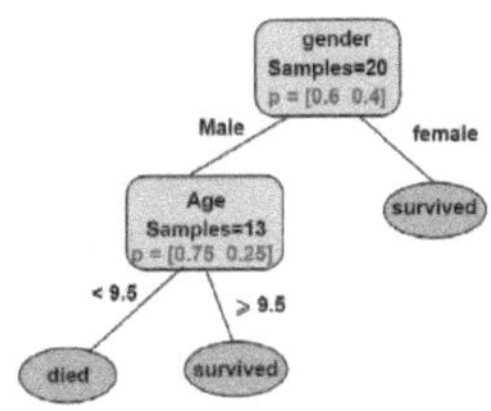

FIGURE 2.2 – the obtained subtree after pruning the weak node.

This novel approach ensures that the tree continues to grow only when the number of samples in a node is sufficiently large and the probability of class membership is notably high, approaching a value close to 1. The specific steps of our developed approach are elucidated in the following algorithm (Algorithm 2.1):

2.1.4 Experiment Results

To test the feasibility of the proposed pruning method, we compared it with the C4.5 algorithm (Quinlan, 1986) and the PBMR algorithm (Pruning with Bayes Minimum Risk) (Ahmed et al., 2018).

2.1.4.1 Datasets

We evaluated the developed approach using 24 binary datasets from the UCI Machine Learning Repository (Asuncion and Newman, 2007). We divided the datasets into small-sized datasets (Table 2.1) and large-sized datasets (Table 2.2). For each dataset, we provide the number of instances, the number of

Algorithm 2.1: The Proposed pre-pruning algorithm

Input: D: The training dataset with labeled instances
α: the weakness threshold
β: the probability threshold
Output: a tree

begin
  BuildTree (D, α, β) **if** *D is pure.* **then**
    return *a node with a corresponding class label*
  end
  if *size(D) $\leq \alpha$ and prob(majority class) $\geq \beta$* **then**
    return *a node with a corresponding class label*
  end
  for *all attributes $a \in D$* **do**
    Compute information-theoretic criteria if we split on a.
  end
  a_{best} = The best attribute according to the above criteria.
  $tree$ = Create a decision node with a_{best} as splitting attribute.
  D_v = Induced sub-datasets from D based on a_{best}.
  for *all D_v* **do**
    $tree_v$ = BuildTree(D_v, α, β)
    Attach $tree_v$ to the corresponding branch of $tree$
  end
  return $tree$
end

numerical attributes, the number of categorical attributes, and the percentage of the minority class. The datasets included represent a wide variety of characteristics.

We performed a ten-times 10-fold cross-validation. The arithmetic mean and the standard deviation of the 100 runs are presented for each dataset. Table 2.3 shows the AUC scores of the compared methods on small-sized datasets, while Table 2.4 shows the AUC scores for the large datasets. The performance of each model was evaluated using the AUC (Area Under the ROC Curve) metric, as the datasets are unbalanced. The best scores for each dataset are boldfaced.

2.1.4.2 Analysis of results

A quick look at the table reveals that the new pruning method outperforms the decision tree algorithm in most datasets, producing the highest AUC score in twenty-one out of twenty-four datasets and yielding an equal score in the remaining three. Compared to the PBMR algorithm, the developed approach exceeds PBMR in sixteen out of twenty-four datasets, with negligible differences in the others. The best performance with the new pruning method is observed in the transfusion, Ad, Pima, liver, sick, sick-euthyroid, and sonar datasets, which are of small to medium sizes.

TABLE 2.1 – Small data sets characteristics

#	data sets	Size	Attributes		% Min Class
			Num	Nom	
1	transfusion	748	4	0	23.8
2	HillValley	606	100	0	49.7
3	Bands	540	18	20	42.2
4	Pima	768	8	0	34.9
5	Liver	345	6	0	42.03
6	sick	2751	6	21	6.1
7	weka	310	6	0	22.3
8	spect	267	44	0	20.6
9	hypothyroid	3163	6	19	4.8
10	Sick-euthyroid	2000	6	19	8.2
11	horse	299	10	17	40.5
12	wpbc	198	33	0	23.7
13	sonar	208	60	0	46.6
14	wdbc	569	31	0	37.3

TABLE 2.2 – Large data sets characteristics

#	data sets	Size	Attributes		% Min Class
			Num	Nom	
15	eighthr	2533	73	0	6.3
16	spambase	4601	57	0	39.4
17	Bank	41190	10	10	11.27
18	ad	3263	1556	0	13.9
19	adult	32561	0	14	24.1
20	caravan	5822	85	0	6.0
21	Connect	67557	0	42	34.2
22	clean	6598	166	0	15.4
23	numerai	96320	21	0	49.5
24	kobe	25697	12	12	44.6

TABLE 2.3 – Benchmarking results for AUC on the small datasets as a performance metric

#	C4.5	PBMR	Our Algorithm
1	70.6 ± 8.5	71.5 ± 7.3	73.8 ± 7.7
2	56.3 ± 6.1	56.3 ± 6.0	56.4 ± 5.6
3	77.3 ± 4.2	78.0 ± 4.2	77.8 ± 4.1
4	80.4 ± 5.0	81.3 ± 4.7	81.9 ± 4.0
5	68.5 ± 7.4	69.3 ± 7.8	70.3 ± 8.2
6	89.2 ± 5.6	91.2 ± 5.8	91.5 ± 4.2
7	89.0 ± 5.9	90.2 ± 4.0	90.0 ± 4.0
8	60.0 ± 10.3	60.5 ± 9.1	60.8 ± 9.7
9	78.0 ± 4.9	78.0 ± 5.1	78.4 ± 5.1
10	87.2 ± 4.5	88.4 ± 4.5	89.0 ± 4.5
11	75.9 ± 8.3	76.1 ± 8.8	76.5 ± 9.3
12	66.8 ± 11.1	69.0 ± 10.9	68.8 ± 10.5
13	78.1 ± 15.3	78.7 ± 13.4	79.1 ± 12.1
14	97.5 ± 1.6	97.5 ± 1.7	97.6 ± 2.2
Mean	76.77	77.57	77.99

TABLE 2.4 – Benchmarking results for AUC on the large datasets as a performance metric

#	C4.5	PBMR	Our Algorithm
15	70.3 ± 5.9	70.5 ± 6.0	70.4 ± 6.0
16	95.5 ± 1.2	95.7 ± 1.2	96.0 ± 1.2
17	83.1 ± 0.7	83.8 ± 0.7	83.5 ± 0.7
18	90.9 ± 1.9	92.1 ± 2.0	92.7 ± 2.3
19	88.1 ± 0.6	88.2 ± 0.7	88.2 ± 0.7
20	73.7 ± 3.2	73.7 ± 3.2	73.7 ± 3.2
21	82.4 ± 0.6	82.4 ± 0.6	82.4 ± 0.6
22	89.3 ± 2.5	90.0 ± 2.2	90.1 ± 2.2
23	52.2 ± 0.4	52.2 ± 0.4	52.2 ± 0.4
24	68.6 ± 1.0	69.0 ± 1.0	68.8 ± 1.0
Mean	79.41	79.76	79.8

This outcome is expected when decision trees are pruned, as removing details potentially caused by noise helps avoid overfitting. However, these results are somewhat indeterministic because it is unclear whether these details are indeed noise-induced. Our pruning method likely performed better because it halts tree growth when the class membership probability is high and the number of instances is low.

2.2 Enhancing weak nodes in decision tree algorithm

2.2.1 Introduction

In a deep decision tree, it's possible to encounter nodes with a limited number of instances. For instance, during the tree-building process, we might come across a node comprising just three instances. Out of these, two are categorized as positive, while one bears a negative label. However, in practice, this small instance count is insufficient for informed decision-making. As a result, the branch stemming from this node lacks statistical significance and shouldn't be included in the final tree structure.

2.2.2 Example illustrating the problem of weak nodes

Here is an illustration of a binary decision tree as an example (Figure 2.3). When given three instances as input, the classifier iterates through the branches based on the conditions met by the split attribute. This traversal continues until a leaf node is reached, which specifies the prediction.

While the classifier appears to perform optimally by dividing the node into two pure subsets, a crucial consideration arises: is the sample size of three instances sufficient for generating a dependable prediction? There exists a possibility that these three instances could be outliers, potentially rendering this specific node of inferior quality. Consequently, this node may fail to generalize effectively and could result in poor predictive capabilities.

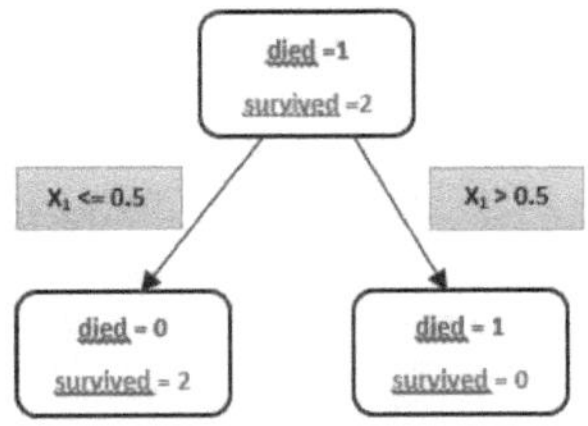

FIGURE 2.3 – Example of node containing three instances

Figure 2.4 represents the graphical representation of the previous graph:

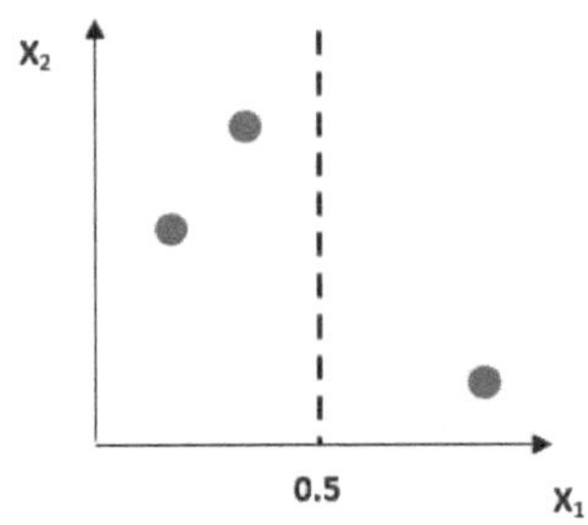

FIGURE 2.4 – The graphical representation of the previous node

Now suppose an individual with a threshold 0.6 labeled positive so this individual will be misclassified with this classifier as shown in Figure 2.5.

This situation is quite normal, as the limited number of instances within the node poses a challenge in accurately predicting class labels for this region. This is why the decision tree tries to predict outcomes for test examples by leveraging other training instances that are not pertinent to the classification task at hand.

To address this, a strategy involves augmenting the data within this node by incorporating data from another similar node. By doing so, the prediction gains enhanced reliability and robustness.

Following the augmentation of data within the node, a subsequent step involves recalculating both the split attribute and the optimal threshold for this attribute. This can entail adjusting the threshold (as depicted in Fig. 2.6) or even modifying the chosen split attribute (as illustrated in Fig. 2.7). Consequently, the node gains increased strength and the decision-making process becomes more dependable, leading to improved overall predictive

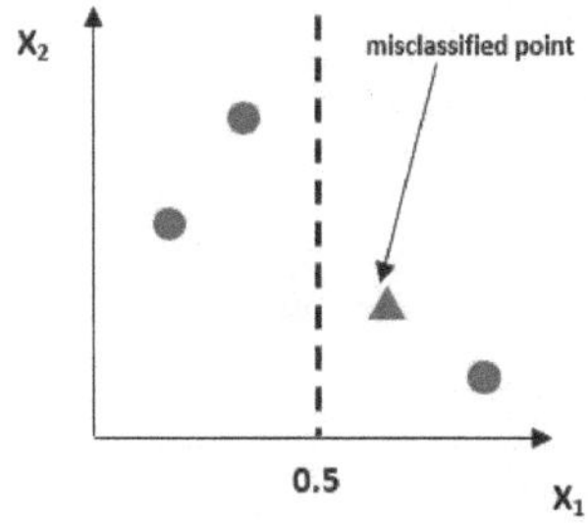

FIGURE 2.5 – Example of misclassification point

performance.

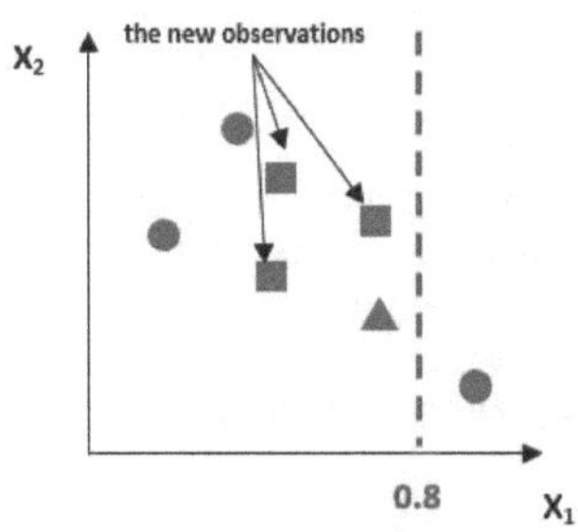

FIGURE 2.6 – the threshold correction of the node after data augmentation

2.2.3 Proposed approach

The EWNDT algorithm represents a modified variant of the C4.5 Algorithm (Quinlan, 1993), implementing a breadth-first methodology. Our primary innovation involves enhancing nodes with limited data, referred to as weak nodes (those having examples below a specified threshold β, for instance, β=5), during the tree construction phase. Whenever a node is categorized as weak, it is not placed within the fringe. Instead, it is designated to a distinct collection termed the $pausedNodeSet$, which encompasses all such weak nodes.

Upon completing the initial tree structure, our focus shifts to processing these weak nodes. We iterate through all nodes in the $pausedNodeSet$. In each iteration, a node N is extracted from the $pausedNodeSet$. Subsequently, we search for nodes similar to N within the already established tree. Once these similar nodes are identified, we merge their data with the ongoing node N and calculate the best splitting attribute and its corresponding threshold. This construction process continues until the collection of weak nodes is exhausted. The mechanics of node similarity are detailed in the subsequent section.

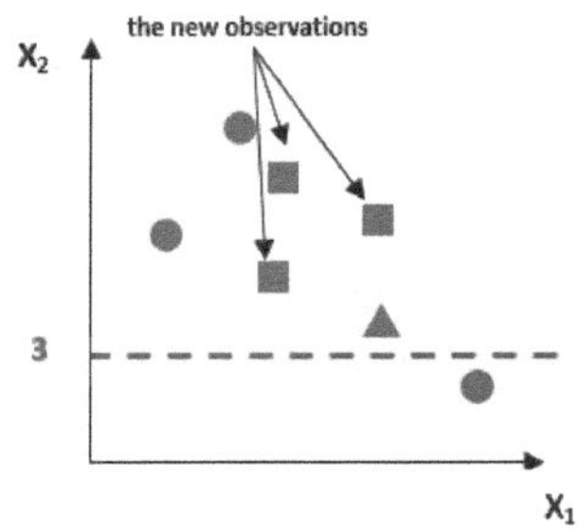

FIGURE 2.7 – the change of split attribute after data augmentation

2.2.3.1 The EWNDT algorithm

The precise step-by-step depiction of our approach is outlined below:

Algorithm 2.2: Create a node

```
Function BuildNode(D, Y):
                ▷ Where D - training data, Y - target attribute;
    if all elements in D belong to the same class label then
        return a node with corresponding class label;
    end
    else if One of the Stopping criteria is fulfilled then
        return node with majority class label in D;
    end
    else
        select Attribute A which best classifies D;
        Mark the node with A as split Attribute;
        if number of instances of the node ≤ β then
            add the new node to the pausedNodeSet;
        end
        else
            add the new node to the fringe;
        end
    end
    return node;
```

The code lines 1 to 22 from the EWNDT algorithm (Algorithm 2.3) represents the classical decision tree algorithm.

2.2.3.2 General conditions of the algorithm

The objective of the EWNDT algorithm is to augment the data of nodes identified as weak by combining their data with that of other comparable nodes.

Algorithm 2.3: The EWNDT Algorithm

```
1  Function EWNDT(D, Y):
2                  ▷ Where D - training data, Y - target attribute;
3      fringe, pausedNodeSet = ∅ // Global variables;
4      if all elements in D belong to the same class label then
5          return a node with corresponding class label;
6      end
7      else if One of the Stopping criteria is fulfilled then
8          return node with majority class label in D;
9      end
10     else
11         select Attribute A which best classifies D;
12         Mark the root node with A as split Attribute;
13         add the root node to the fringe;
14         while the fringe is not empty do
15             pop node n from the fringe;
16             splitA = n.splitAttribute;
17             for each possible value v of splitA do
18                 sub = subset of D that have value v for splitA;
19                 n.addBranch(BuildNode (Dsub ,Ysub));
20             end
21         end
22     end
23     while the pausedNodeSet is not empty do
24         pop node N from the pausedNodeSet;
25         find similar nodes to N;
26         if more than one node is similar to N then
27             CN = the node that has the minimum distance to N;
28             merge the data of N and CN and return to line 8;
29         end
30         else
31             SN = the similar node to N;
32             merge the data of N and SN and return to line 8;
33         end
34     end
35     return root;
```

This merging of data is conducted in a virtual manner to establish the optimal splitting attribute and threshold. As this supplementary data isn't retained within the child nodes, certain conditions must be validated before the merging process. The conditions that need to be verified are as follows:

- Two nodes belonging to the same branch (nodes on the same path from the tree root to a leaf node (Fig. 2.8)) cannot be merged.

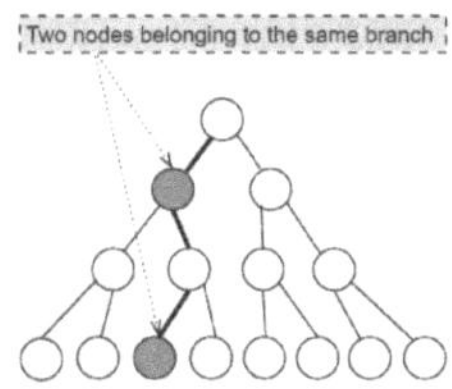

FIGURE 2.8 – Example of two nodes belonging to the same branch

- Two sibling nodes (nodes with the same parent node (Fig. 2.9)) cannot be merged.

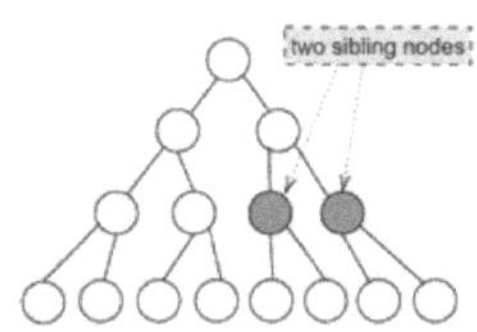

FIGURE 2.9 – Example of two sibling nodes

- When multiple nodes similar to the current one are encountered, the nearest node is selected (for instance, the node with the smallest distance from the current node). The procedure to compute the distance between two nodes is explained in the subsequent subsection.
- In scenarios where more than one similar node to the current one is discovered and these similar nodes are positioned equidistant from the current node, the data from all these nodes is combined with the current one. This fusion aims to facilitate the selection of a more dependable splitting attribute.

2.2.3.3 Distance between two nodes

The distance d between two nodes n_1 and n_2 is the minimum number of edges traversed from n_1 to n_2. It is calculated using the following formula:

$$d = (n_1.depth - ca.depth) + (n_2.depth - ca.depth) \tag{2.1}$$

where ca is the common ancestor of the two nodes (i.e., the common node between the two branches carrying these two nodes). The distance between two nodes n_1 and n_2 can be computed as the distance from n_1 to ca, plus the distance from ca to n_2. Fig. 2.10 explains the method to calculate the distance between two nodes.

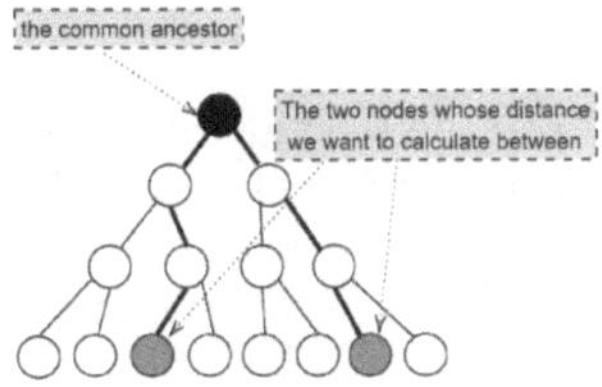

FIGURE 2.10 – Figure illustrating the method of calculating the distance between two nodes

2.2.3.4 Node Similarity

To merge two nodes in the tree, they must be similar, but there are several similarity criteria. We have used two approaches for comparing the similarity of the nodes:

2.2.3.4.1 Treshold Approach : Two nodes n_1 and n_2 in the tree are similar if they satisfy the following conditions:

- if they have the same split attribute
- if they are labeled with the same class
- if ($| n_1.thresh - n_2.thresh | \leq simThresh$)

where $n_1.thresh$ and $n_2.thresh$ are the thresholds that give the best distribution of data in each node. $simThresh$ is a parameter that measures the closeness between two thresholds (e.g., if $simThresh = 0.1$, two thresholds are considered equal if their difference is less than 0.1). The thresholds of every $i - th$ splitting attribute z_i are normalized (i.e., its values are between 0 and 1) using the following formula:

$$z_i = \frac{x_i - x_{min}}{x_{max} - x_{min}} \quad (2.2)$$

where $x = (x_1, ..., x_n)$ is the data before normalization, x_{max} is the maximum value for the attribute x_i, x_{min} is the minimum value for the attribute x_i, and z_i is now the $i - th$ normalized data. We normalized the thresholds to facilitate the detection of similar ones to be generalized for the whole attribute space. In the case where thresholds are unnormalized, a simThresh value must be determined for each attribute. Two nodes, n_1 and n_2, in the tree are similar in the case of categorical attributes if they satisfy the following conditions:

- if they have the same split attribute
- if they are labeled with the same class

- The difference between their predictability is less than a threshold α (Hu et al., 2009),

where the predictability of a node N is defined as a conditional probability:

$$predictability(N) = prob(N.splitAttr = N.thresh|N.label) \quad (2.3)$$

where $N.splitAttr$ and $N.thresh$ are the best attribute and threshold values to split the node N while $N.label$ represents the class label with the majority vote in the node N. For example, let's take $\alpha = 0.1$. Two nodes n_1 and n_2 are merged if:

$$\mid predictability(n_1) - predictability(n_2) \mid \leq 0.1. \quad (2.4)$$

We only compute the predictability when the first two conditions are verified, i.e., we calculate predictability when the two nodes have the same class and the same splitting attribute.

2.2.3.4.2 Probabilistic approach : This method treats numerical and categorical attributes equally by relying on predicted class probabilities, which signify the proportion of samples belonging to a particular class within a node. To illustrate how class probabilities are interpreted, let's consider an example of a node containing five instances: two with positive labels and three with negative labels. Consequently, the probability of the positive class is 2/5 = 0.4, while the probability of the negative class is 3/5 = 0.6. Two nodes within a decision tree are deemed similar when they meet the following criteria:

- if they have the same splitting attribute
- if($\mid n_1.prob - n_2.prob \mid \leq probThresh$)
  $probThresh$ is a parameter that measures the similarity between two probabilities (e.g. if $probTresh$=0.1, two probabilities are considered similar if their difference is less than 0.1)

2.2.3.5 The strengths and limitations of the developed approach

When the tree's depth is high, there is a risk of having very few data points in the terminal nodes, which can lead to unreliable predictions for future cases, resulting in low generalizability. To address this issue, we enhance the data in these nodes by augmenting their data from similar nodes. This novel approach enables the construction of a reliable and robust decision tree with improved accuracy. We have empirically tested the validity of our proposal and showcased its advantages through practical examples and comparative analyses. The results discussion demonstrates its usability and strengths compared to existing methods. However, the EWNDT algorithm does have some drawbacks in comparison to other approaches, with the primary limitation being the substantial time it takes to construct the tree on all datasets, resulting in slightly more complex trees.

2.2.3.6 Time Complexity of the algorithm

It is true the new algorithm indeed builds more complex trees, but they are more relevant to the previous one. To evaluate the time complexity of our algorithm, we start by calculating the complexity of each step. First, we consider the time complexity of the technique used of searching the best split.This technique consists of sorting the data into ascending order along with that data point. Then consider all possible partition points between those data points and taking the one that minimizes the entropy. This sorting step takes time $O(n * log(n))$. Since we are doing that for each of the $O(m)$ features, the total time complexity would be $O(m * nlog(n))$.Finally, we will repeat this process for all weak nodes whose number is w then the final complexity will be $O(m * nlog(n) * w)$.

2.2.4 Evaluation and validation

2.2.4.1 Datasets

To evaluate the performance of the proposed algorithm, experiments were performed using twenty real-world datasets from the UCI repository. All of them have two classes; Table 2.5 shows the dataset, the size, the number of nominal and numerical attributes and the percentage of examples of the minority class.

TABLE 2.5 – Data sets characteristics

#	data sets	Size	Attributes		% Min Class
			Num	Nom	
1	Transfusion	748	4	0	23.8
2	eighthr	2533	73	0	6.3
3	spambase	4601	57	0	39.4
4	Bank	41190	10	10	11.3
5	Hill valley	606	100	0	49.7
6	ad	3263	1556	0	13.9
7	cyl bands	540	18	20	42.2
8	Pima	768	8	0	34.9
9	adult	32561	0	14	24.1
10	Caravan	5822	85	0	6.0
11	Connect 2c	67557	0	42	34.2
12	Liver	345	6	0	42.0
13	clean	6598	166	0	15.4
14	sick	2751	6	21	6.1
15	weka	310	6	0	22.3
16	spect	267	44	0	20.6
17	hypothyroid	3163	6	19	4.8
18	numerai	96320	21	0	49.5
19	kobr bryant	25697	12	12	44.6
20	sick-euthyroid	2000	6	19	8.2

2.2.4.2 Parameters tuning

The following table summarizes the optimal parameters for each dataset used in our method, ENWDT, with two approaches: ENWDT with threshold similarity (ENWDTT) and ENWDT with probability similarity (ENWDTP), as well as the C4.5 method. For each dataset, we present the maximum tree depth, the number of nodes in the constructed tree, and β, which represents the weakness indicator of the current node

TABLE 2.6 – Optimal parameters for EWNDT and C4.5 for each dataset

Method	Data set	Depth	β	Nbr of nodes	Data set	Depth	β	Nbr of nodes
C4.5		5	#	31		9	#	423
EWNDTT	1	7	20	38	11	9	10	398
EWNDTP		7	20	37		9	10	403
C4.5		3	#	18		9	#	39
EWNDTT	2	4	30	21	12	9	20	37
EWNDTP		4	30	23		9	20	36
C4.5		6	#	45		9	#	84
EWNDTT	3	7	50	48	13	9	50	82
EWNDTP		7	50	48		9	50	81
C4.5		7	#	110		8	#	27
EWNDTT	4	7	50	107	14	8	50	27
EWNDTP		7	50	106		8	50	27
C4.5		8	#	19		3	#	6
EWNDTT	5	9	50	18	15	3	50	6
EWNDTP		9	50	20		3	50	6
C4.5		5	#	31		9	#	19
EWNDTT	6	7	20	38	16	9	20	21
EWNDTP		7	20	37		9	20	22
C4.5		3	#	18		9	#	25
EWNDTT	7	4	30	21	17	9	50	24
EWNDTP		4	30	23		9	50	26
C4.5		5	#	25		7	#	293
EWNDTT	8	5	30	23	18	7	50	271
EWNDTP		5	30	22		7	50	273
C4.5		9	#	193		9	#	166
EWNDTT	9	9	50	171	19	9	50	171
EWNDTP		9	50	175		9	50	172
C4.5		4	#	13		9	#	26
EWNDTT	10	4	50	12	20	9	50	21
EWNDTP		4	50	12		9	50	24

According to table 2.6, trees generated by EWNDT are much smaller than those generated by C4.5 in 11 of the 20 data sets. This can be explained by the fact that the data augmentation in weak nodes by similar data allows the classifier to quickly find pure nodes.

2.2.5 Results and discussion

2.2.5.1 Results

We have compared our two approaches (EWNDT with threshold Similarity (**ENWDTT**) and EWNDT with probability Similarity (**ENWDTP**)) with four state-of-the-art decision tree methods. We performed 10-fold cross-validation. In what follows, for each dataset, we show the arithmetic mean and the standard deviation of the 10 runs.
Table 2.7 presents the results of our benchmarking. The performance of each model has been evaluated using the AUC metric (area under the roc curve). We have used the AUC as a performance metric because the datasets used here have different distributions and most of them are unbalanced.
The best scores for each dataset are boldfaced.

TABLE 2.7 – Evaluation of the two proposed approaches vs. four state-of-the-art decision tree algorithms.

D. sets	C4.5	EWNDTT	EWNDTP	QUEST	CHAID	CART
1	70.6 ± 8.5	**71.9 ± 8.4**	**71.9 ± 7.4**	71.1 ± 5.1	71.0 ± 6.0	71.5 ± 8.6
2	70.3 ± 5.9	70.3 ± 5.9	**70.4 ± 5.9**	70.2 ± 5.7	70.1 ± 5.9	**70.4 ± 5.8**
3	95.5 ± 1.2	95.5 ± 1.2	95.7 ± 1.2	95.8 ± 1.3	**95.9 ± 1.2**	95.7 ± 1.1
4	83.1 ± 0.7	83.3 ± 0.8	83.7 ± 0.8	**84.1 ± 0.7**	83.2 ± 0.8	83.7 ± 0.8
5	56.3 ± 6.1	56.6 ± 4.5	56.3 ± 6.1	55.3 ± 5.1	**58.6 ± 4.7**	57.2 ± 6.1
6	90.9 ± 1.9	91.3 ± 1.6	91.4 ± 1.6	91.8 ± 1.9	91.7 ± 1.6	**92.4 ± 1.5**
7	77.3 ± 4.2	**78.3 ± 4.2**	78.0 ± 4.5	77.3 ± 4.1	**78.3 ± 4.2**	78.0 ± 4.4
8	80.4 ± 5.0	**82.4 ± 4.5**	**82.4 ± 4.0**	81.1 ± 5.0	80.9 ± 4.7	81.6 ± 4.0
9	88.1 ± 0.6	88.2 ± 0.6	**89.7 ± 0.6**	86.1 ± 0.7	85.2 ± 0.9	87.7 ± 0.6
10	73.7 ± 3.2	73.7 ± 3.2	73.7 ± 3.2	73.1 ± 3.2	73.7 ± 3.2	73.2 ± 3.2
11	82.4 ± 0.6	82.4 ± 0.6	82.4 ± 0.6	82.4 ± 0.6	82.4 ± 0.6	82.2 ± 0.6
12	68.5 ± 7.4	**72.6 ± 5.7**	71.8 ± 7.1	69.8 ± 7.3	70.5 ± 6.7	71.7 ± 7.1
13	89.3 ± 2.5	89.4 ± 2.5	89.8 ± 2.4	89.9 ± 2.7	90.3 ± 2.8	**90.7 ± 2.4**
14	89.2 ± 5.6	**90.4 ± 4.0**	**90.4 ± 4.0**	89.6 ± 4.6	90.1 ± 5.0	90.2 ± 5.2
15	89.0 ± 5.9	**89.5 ± 6.0**	**89.5 ± 6.0**	89.1 ± 5.8	88.7 ± 6.1	88.9 ± 6.0
16	60.0 ± 10.3	61.2 ± 10.6	62.3 ± 9.9	**63.0 ± 10.1**	62.3 ± 10.2	62.5 ± 9.9
17	78.0 ± 4.9	78.0 ± 4.9	79.0 ± 5.0	78.5 ± 4.8	78.2 ± 4.9	**79.1 ± 5.0**
18	52.2 ± 0.4	52.2 ± 0.4	52.2 ± 0.4	**53.0 ± 0.6**	51.7 ± 0.5	52.5 ± 0.5
19	68.6 ± 1.0	68.7 ± 1.0	68.7 ± 1.0	68.9 ± 1.2	69.3 ± 1.4	**69.6 ± 1.1**
20	87.2 ± 4.5	88.9 ± 5.6	**89.1 ± 4.9**	87.2 ± 4.7	88.9 ± 5.2	**89.1 ± 5.9**
Mean	77.5	78.2	**78.4**	77.9	78.0	**78.4**

2.2.5.2 Analysis of results

According to table 2.7, the EWNDT algorithm with threshold similarity outperformed all the other methods with six (transfusion, bands, pima, sick weka, and liver) of the twenty datasets while the difference between EWNDT and the other method in the remaining datasets is small. The second approach that uses probability's similarity outperforms all the other methods in seven of the twenty datasets. As we can see, the common factor between the datasets where our algorithm outperforms the other methods is that they have a few attributes. The first approach gives the best performance in numerical data sets, although the second approach does not differentiate between types of datasets. But generally, the second approach gives the best performance compared to the other methods.

2.2.6 Summary of the chapter

The first finding presents a new pruning method based on the decision tree algorithm, which stops the tree's growth when the number of examples in a decision node is minimum, and the probability of belonging to the target attribute is highest. Experimental evaluation has shown that the method is efficient and accurate compared to the decision tree algorithm and the PBMR algorithm in terms of the AUC metric. In future work, we will investigate the same pruning method to see how we can provide users with more flexibility in incorporating domain-specific knowledge into decision trees to achieve optimal prediction results.

The second finding presented a new algorithm based on the Decision Tree Algorithm, which reinforces weak nodes in the tree by augmenting its data from other similar nodes using two similarity approaches. The first approach uses threshold similarity for the numerical attribute and the conditional probability for the categorical attribute. The similarity criterion by the second approach uses node distribution. We have compared our method to four state-of-the-art decision tree methods (C4.5, CART, QUEST, and CHAID) which are the most popular ones. Therefore, the experimental results demonstrated that the new algorithm has fewer leaf nodes and higher classification performance.

There are at least two areas for immediate future exploration for the second paper. First, we consider only the binary class in our experiment. And the problem may be more complex if a non-binary class is considered. The second direction is to search other similarity criteria between nodes. One more direction is in the case we found more than one node similar to the current node we chose here the node that has the minimum distance to the current node so other approaches could be applied here.

Chapter 3

KNN based methods

Contents

The first study proposes an improved KNN ensemble method using a correlation-based feature subselection technique. The new algorithm builds an ensemble of KNN models and aggregates their predictions to form the final predictions. This approach offers potential advantages: first, it reduces the memory space used by the algorithm by employing a simple subset of features at each iteration; Second, a performance improvement is possible since the ensemble prediction exceeds that of an individual estimator. The second study introduces an innovative feature weighting approach tailored to enhancing the performance of the KNN algorithm. This novel weighting technique merges the strengths of association rules and information gains to allocate weights to individual features within a dataset, taking into account the target attribute. The suggested method demonstrates superior performance when compared to similar approaches.

3.1 An improved KNN algorithm based on ensemble methods and correlation

3.1.1 Introduction

Ensemble methods seek to enhance a model's predictive capabilities by combining the outputs of multiple models. In the case of K-Nearest Neighbors (KNN) ensemble methods, this principle is applied to KNN models, forming an ensemble of KNN classifiers or regressors. Each individual KNN model is trained using a portion of the training data or with varying parameter configurations, yielding a collection of diverse models. Ensemble methods based on K-Nearest Neighbors (KNN) can pose significant computational challenges, especially when handling extensive datasets or feature spaces with high dimensionality. Addressing these challenges and enhancing scalability is an active field of research. Possible strategies to achieve this may involve the development of efficient algorithms and optimization techniques. These methods could encompass approaches like data reduction, instance selection, or parallelization of the ensemble construction process. Hence, in light of these challenges, we introduce an enhanced K-Nearest Neighbors (KNN) ensemble method that incorporates a feature subselection approach grounded in correlation analysis. This novel algorithm assembles a collection of KNN models and subsequently combines their predictions to yield the ultimate predictions.

3.1.2 Developed approach

Our proposed ensemble method employs K-Nearest Neighbors (KNN) as the base learner. Here's a breakdown of the algorithm:

1. **Bootstrap Sampling**: We begin by generating N bootstrap examples from the initial dataset, using a process that allows examples to be selected with replacement.
2. **Feature Correlation Analysis**: For each subset of these bootstrapped examples, we calculate the correlation between each feature and the target attribute. Only the features exhibiting a positive correlation with the target attribute are retained.

3. **Selective KNN**: Using the selected features, we then employ KNN to find the k-nearest neighbors for unlabeled test examples. During this process, only the chosen subset of features is utilized in calculating the Euclidean distances.
4. **Prediction Aggregation**: Finally, we aggregate the predictions from the KNN models using a majority voting scheme.

The following flowchart visually represents the steps of this proposed algorithm:

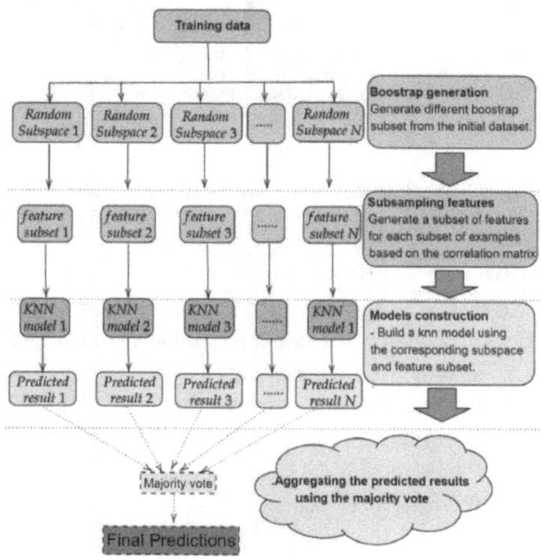

FIGURE 3.1 – Flowchart of the developed approach.

3.1.2.1 Example of correlation calculation between features

Using the correlation matrix illustrated in Figure 3.2 as an example, our primary focus centers on comprehending the relationships between different attributes and the target attribute, denoted as 'y.' A careful examination of the correlation matrix reveals that there is a positive correlation between 'X1' and 'X3,' whereas 'X2' does not exhibit such a correlation. As a result, for this dataset, we will opt to retain 'X1' and 'X3,' and utilize them in the calculation of the Euclidean distance for identifying the k nearest neighbors.

The exact process of the developed approach is described in the following algorithm:

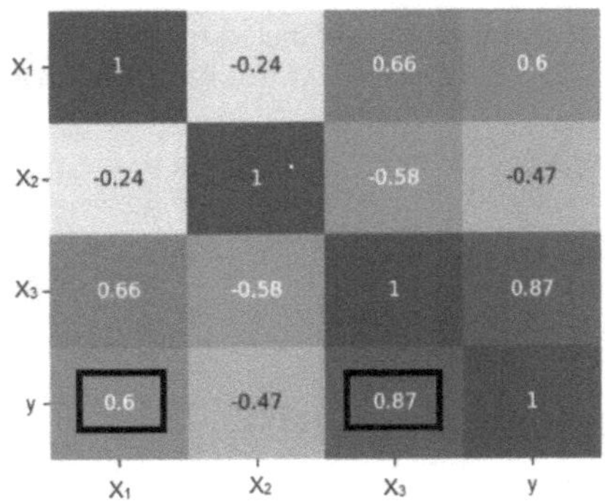

FIGURE 3.2 – Example of a correlation matrix.

Algorithm 3.1: The developed approach algorithm

Input: $trainData$: The training dataset with labeled instances
$testData$: The instances for which we want to make a prediction
k: The number of nearest neighbors to consider
N: The number of KNN classifiers in the ensemble
Output: predictions: The predicted class label for the $testData$

begin
    Function `KnnEnsemble` ($trainData, testData, k, N$):
        $predictions = \emptyset$
        for i = *1 to* N **do**
            d_i = randomly sample $trainData$ with replacement
            $features$ = select features that positively correlate with the target attribute according to d_i
            $classifierKnn = KNN(trainData, k, features)$
            $preds[i] = classifierKnn.predict(testData)$
        end
        $predictions = MajorityVote(preds)$
        return *predictions*
end

Here are the main steps of the developed approach:

- **Step 1**: Generate N subsets selected randomly with replacement from the initial dataset using the bootstrap method.
- **Step 2**: Generate the correlation matrix on each subset of the training set. And eliminate features whose correlation with target attributes are negative.
- **Step 3**: Train multiple k-NN classifiers on each subset of the training set. Each classifier may be trained on a different subset of features.
- **Step 4**: Combine the predictions of the k-NN classifiers to make a final prediction using the majority vote.

- **Step 5**: tune the hyperparameters of the k-NN classifiers or the ensemble method itself using the cross-validation technique.
- **Step 6**: Use the trained ensemble classifier to make predictions on new unseen data

3.1.2.2 Advantages and drawbacks of the developed approach

The developed approach can bring several benefits, such as:

- Improved accuracy: feature weighting can increase KNN accuracy by emphasizing the most important characteristics. This is especially beneficial when working with datasets containing multiple characteristics, some of which may be less informative than others.
- Reduction in Dimensionality: By using only a subset of features, the ensemble method can reduce the dimensionality of the dataset. This can be particularly beneficial when dealing with high-dimensional data, as it can help mitigate the "curse of dimensionality" and improve computational efficiency.
- Increased efficiency: by lowering the number of irrelevant characteristics utilized in the distance computation, feature weighting can further increase the efficiency of KNN. KNN can save needless calculations and lower the algorithm's computational cost by assigning a weight of zero to non-informative features.
- Flexibility: the number of selected attributes varies according to the subset of examples, which increases the diversity of the created models and, consequently, their accuracy.

Despite its usefulness, the developed approach (PM) has some limitations when compared to other methods, such as:

- **Information Loss**: Using only a subset of features can lead to information loss, especially if important features are excluded. This may result in less accurate predictions, particularly when missing relevant features.
- **Optimal Subset Selection**: Determining the best subset of features can be challenging. The ensemble method must have a robust mechanism to identify the most relevant features to include, which can require additional computation and careful tuning

3.1.2.3 Algorithm complexity

3.1.2.3.1 The complexity of a KNN ensemble method (using all features):

Suppose the original dataset has n data points, and the full feature set has d dimensions (features). - In the classic KNN ensemble method (KNNEM) algorithm, where all features are used to calculate the Euclidean distance, the time complexity for computing the distance for a single data point is $O(d)$.
- Therefore, the time complexity for predicting a single data point using classic KNNEM is $O(d)$.
- The overall time complexity for predicting all data points in the dataset is $O(n * d)$, where n is the number of data points.

3.1.2.3.2 The complexity of the developed approach - The ensemble method selects a subset of features of size k (where $k << d$), and the complexity of computing the Euclidean distance for a single data point reduces from $O(d)$ to $O(k)$, where k is the number of selected features.
- Therefore, the time complexity for predicting a single data point using this ensemble method is $O(k)$ instead of the traditional $O(d)$ in the standard KNNEM algorithm.
- The overall time complexity for predicting all data points in the dataset remains $O(n * k)$, where n is the number of data points.

3.1.2.3.3 Comparison The developed approach has a reduced time complexity of $O(k)$ per prediction compared to the classic KNNEM's $O(d)$ per prediction when k is much smaller than d.
If the selected subset size, k, is significantly smaller than the total number of features, d, the ensemble method can be computationally more efficient than the classic KNNEM. The reduction in time complexity becomes more pronounced as the number of features in the original dataset increases.

3.1.3 Evaluation

To assess the viability of the suggested approach, we carried out a comparative examination against various alternative algorithms. More precisely, we evaluated how well the developed approach performed when compared to the K-nearest neighbors (KNN) algorithm Cover and Hart (1967a), the Approximate Nearest Neighbor (ANN) algorithm (Mehanovic et al., 2020), and the Ensemble Method of KNN (EMKNN) (Kohavi and John, 1997).

3.1.3.1 Datasets

To evaluate the efficiency of the suggested approach, we performed experiments on fifteen real-world datasets, all of which were publicly accessible from the UCI repository (Asuncion and Newman, 2007) and Kaggle (Kaggle, 2024). Table 3.1 offers a comprehensive overview of these datasets, all of which entailed binary classification tasks. We showed the size of each dataset, as well as the count of nominal and numerical attributes associated with them.

3.1.3.2 Results of the experiments

To achieve the results, each dataset undergoes five cross-validations. Five models are generated from each training dataset in our experiments, and their performance is evaluated against the corresponding test datasets. The reported performances in the figures below represent the average of the five folds. Figure 3.3 illustrates the accuracy outcomes of our developed approach in comparison to other algorithms, while Figure 3.4 presents precision scores, and Figure 3.5 showcases the evaluation of the methods in terms of Recall.

TABLE 3.1 – Data sets characteristics

#	data sets	Size	Attributes	
			Num	Nom
1	Heart	303	6	7
2	Bands	540	24	15
3	Hepatitis	129	6	13
4	Titanic	1307	2	24
5	Spect	267	44	6
6	Sonar	208	60	0
7	Wdbc	569	30	0
8	HillValey	606	100	0
9	Magic04	19020	10	0
10	Eighthr	2533	73	0
11	Clean	6598	168	0
12	Eye	14980	14	0
13	Ionosphere	351	14	0
14	CreditCards	30000	24	0
15	Pima	768	8	0

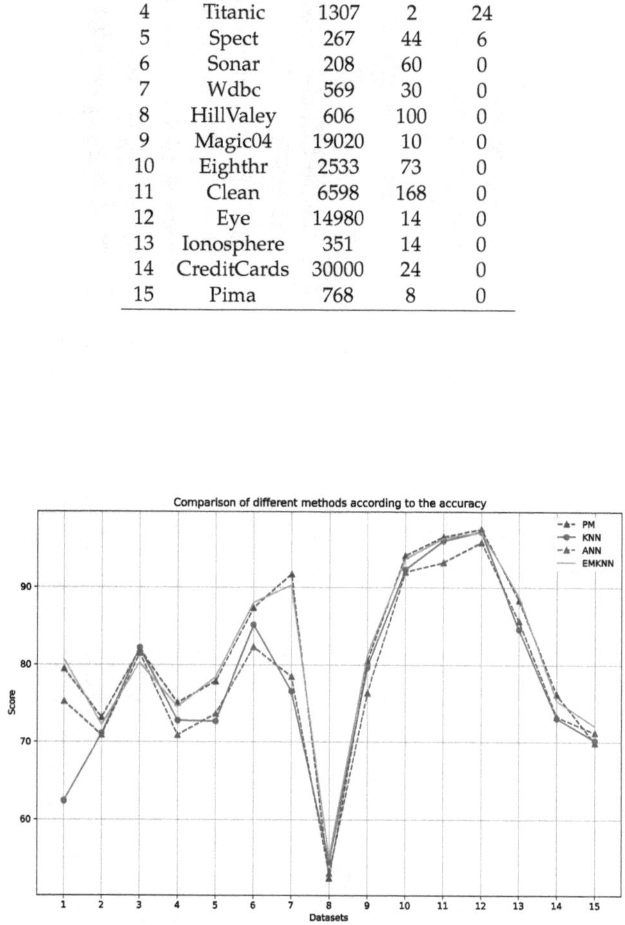

FIGURE 3.3 – The performance of the developed approach compared to the SOTA algorithms according to the accuracy.

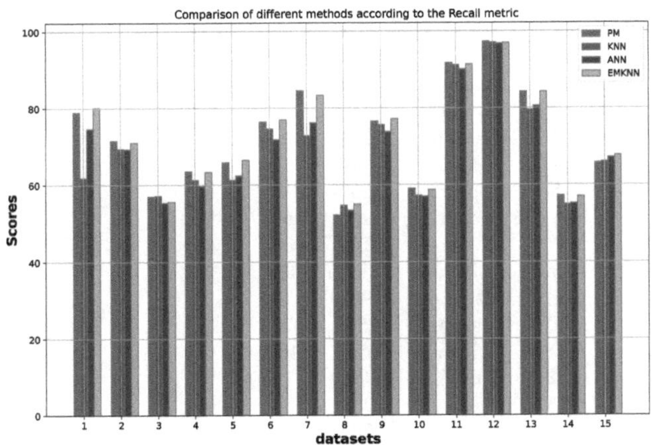

FIGURE 3.4 – The performance of the developed approach compared to the SOTA algorithms according to the Recall metric.

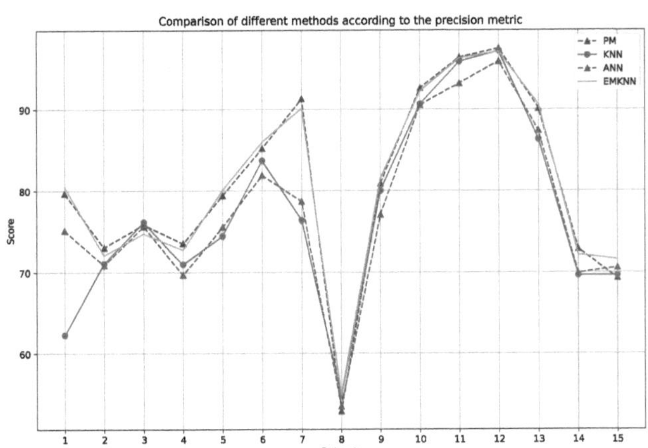

FIGURE 3.5 – The performance of the developed approach compared to the SOTA algorithms according to the precision metric.

3.1.3.3 Analysis of the results

Fig 3.3 indicates that the developed approach surpasses its competitors in seven out of fifteen datasets, with only minor variations in performance for the remaining datasets. Consequently, when considering average accuracy across all datasets, both the developed approach and EMKNN exhibit the highest performance. Examining Fig 3.4, the developed approach consistently demonstrates strong performance in most datasets, achieving the highest precision in 'Bands,' 'wdbc,' and 'credit cards.' Turning to Fig 3.5, the developed approach excels in recall performance across numerous datasets, particularly 'Bands,' 'wdbc,' and 'eighthr.' Overall, the developed approach exhibits superior performance across all three performance metrics in comparison to most other methods, with a slight advantage over EMKNN, where its performance is nearly equivalent but slightly favorable.

3.2 An improved KNN algorithm based on feature weighting and association rules

3.2.1 Introduction

The K-nearest neighbors (KNN) algorithm relies on feature weighting to enhance its accuracy by acknowledging that not all dataset elements are equally important for classifying data points. Feature weighting assigns significance to dataset features using techniques like mutual information, correlation-based feature selection, or chi-square feature selection. These weights guide distance calculations, often using Euclidean distance as a metric, to better capture the data's structure and improve predictions, particularly in high-dimensional datasets.

Various distance metrics, including Euclidean distance, L1-norm distance, χ^2 distance, and Mahalanobis distance, are used for classification, both with and without learning. Learning-based distances like Xing distance, Information Theoretic Metric Learning (ITML)-based distance, Kernel Relevant Component Analysis (KRCA), Large Margin Nearest Neighbour (LMNN), and Information Geometric Metric Learning (IGML)-based linear metric can enhance generalization capabilities.

This study introduces a novel feature weighting approach tailored for KNN. It combines association rules and information gains to assign weights to dataset features, considering the target attribute, thereby improving the algorithm's performance.

3.2.2 developed approach

3.2.2.1 Feature weighting importance

We can demonstrate the effectiveness of the feature weighting in the KNN algorithm through the following illustrative example. Consider a two-dimensional classification problem involving three classes, labeled as R, B, and G, as indicated in the legends shown in Figure 3.6.

Two test examples are selected, one from class R and one from class B. In the absence of class-specific feature weighting, the k-nearest neighbors (kNN) algorithm with Euclidean distance will incorrectly assign both test points to class G, as depicted in Figure 3.7.

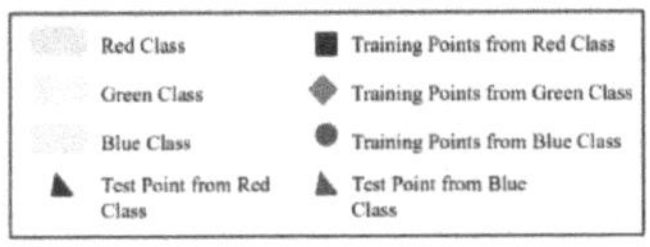

FIGURE 3.6 – Legends used in Fig. 3.7 and Fig. 3.8

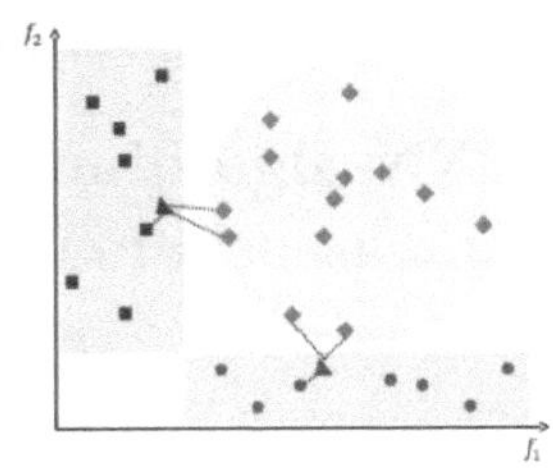

FIGURE 3.7 – Classification with KNN using Euclidian distance without feature weighting.

However, upon closer examination, it becomes evident that feature f_2 does not significantly contribute to identifying a member of class R, while feature f_1 plays a crucial role in discerning class B. Therefore, employing a weighted Euclidean distance metric could prove beneficial.

As illustrated in Figure 3.8, it becomes apparent that applying these weightings appropriately categorizes both test points into their respective classes. Consequently, this approach aims to enhance accuracy.

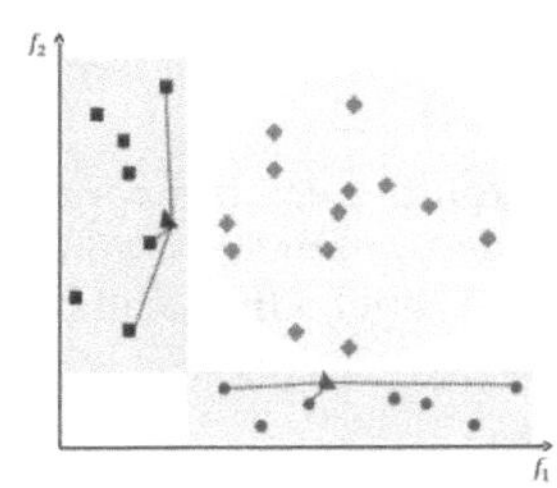

FIGURE 3.8 – Classification with KNN using Euclidian distance with feature weighting.

3.2.2.2 Motivation

Our motivation stems from the recognition that the performance of the K-nearest neighbors (KNN) algorithm can be enhanced through the use of appropriate feature weighting. Given that association rules are an effective means of uncovering dependencies between two data items, it naturally follows that they can gauge the relationships between each feature and the target attribute. Consequently, we were confident that their incorporation into the feature weighting process would be advantageous.

In addition, information gain quantifies the amount of information a feature contributes to class differentiation. By evaluating the Gain of each variable in relation to the target variable, information gain can also serve as a tool for feature selection. Thus, the combination of these two techniques to estimate feature weights for the KNN algorithm holds promise for improved classification performance. This can be achieved by determining a set of globally optimized weights for the features.

3.2.2.3 The main finding

This section describes the theoretical basis behind the proposed KNN classifier. In particular, we propose a new feature weighting technique based on two criteria association rules and information gain. The following flowchart (Fig. 3.9) describes the process of the developed approach: First, we generate

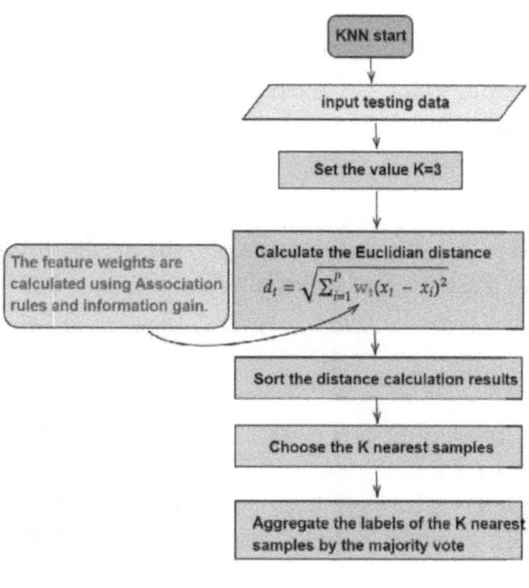

FIGURE 3.9 – Flowchart of the developed approach.

association rules using the Apriori algorithm; then, we select the rules with output in the consequent. Next, we iterate over these rules and calculate the mean support for each feature. Finally, we calculate information gain for each feature. The proposed feature weighting technique is calculated using the following formula:

$$W(f) = Gain(f) + meanSupp(f) \tag{3.1}$$

Where f represents the feature for which we want to calculate the weight, $Gain(f)$ is the information gain of the feature f, and $meanSupp(f)$ is the mean support of the same feature. The main steps of the proposed feature weighting algorithm are described in detail as follows.

- **Step 1:** Transform all the numerical attributes to intervals in the training Set D.
- **Step 2:** Use the Apriori algorithm to generate an ensemble of association-rule called RS.
- **Step 3:** Identify all the rules with consequences as the output feature from the rule set RS, and then create a new rule set RS_{output} with these rules;
- **Step 4:** Create a new rule set RSS_{output} by eliminating the rules with support less than a given threshold and eliminating all the subsets;
- **Step 5:** Sort RSS_{output} by confidence in descending order first, lift in descending order, and support in descending order last.
- **Step 6:** Iterate over all the rules in RSS_{output} and calculate the average support of each feature. For each attribute a_i, we identify the rules from RSS_{output} where a_i appears, add the support of these rules, and then divide it by the number of times a_i appears in RSS_{output}.
- **Step 7:** Calculate the information gain for each attribute.
- **Step 8:** Calculate the importance of each attribute by adding its information gain and average support.

3.2.3 Experiments

This experiment performed five-fold cross-validation on twenty-five classification problems to compare the different algorithms using four performance criteria.

3.2.3.1 Data sets

The experiment employed twenty-five separate datasets collected without change from the UCI Repository (Asuncion and Newman, 2007) and Kaggle. Table 3.2 displays the datasets' features, which include both continuous and discrete features, the number of samples, and the number of classes.

3.2.3.2 Results of the experiments

The classification performance of our developed approach is assessed by comparing it with various state-of-the-art (SOTA) algorithms, including KNN (Cover and Hart, 1967a), MIFW (Feature Weighting using Mutual Information)(Garcia-Laencina et al., 2009), FKNN for Fuzzy-kNN (Derrac et al., 2014), ENN (Extended Nearest Neighbor) (Tang and He, 2015), DE4

TABLE 3.2 – Datasets descriptions

Id	Name	Characteristics			
		Size	Features	Classes	Type of data
1	Ecoli	366	8	8	both
2	Yeast	1484	9	10	both
3	vowel	990	13	10	Num
4	balance	625	4	3	Num
5	Vehicle	846	18	4	Num
6	heart	303	13	2	Both
7	wine	4898	11	10	Num
8	hepatitis	129	19	2	Both
9	titanic	1307	26	2	both
10	bands	540	38	2	Both
11	Pima	768	8	2	Num
12	sick	2800	29	2	both
13	pendigits	10932	16	10	both
14	ionosphere	351	14	2	Num
15	caravan	5822	85	2	Cat
16	spect	267	44	2	Num
17	eighthr	2533	73	2	Both
18	magic	19020	10	2	Num
19	eye	14980	14	2	Num
20	hillValley	606	100	2	Num
21	credit	30000	24	2	Both
22	clean	6598	168	2	Num
23	wdbc	570	31	2	both
24	madelon	2000	500	2	Num
25	bank	41190	20	2	both

(AlSukker et al., 2010), and Parameter Independent Fuzzy class-specific Feature Weighted KNN (PIFW) (Biswas et al., 2018). This evaluation is conducted using different performance metrics.

To ensure robust results, we perform five-fold cross-validation on each dataset. During this process, we create five distinct models from the training dataset and subsequently evaluate their performance against their respective test datasets. The reported performance metrics in the following tables represent the averages obtained across these five folds.

Table 3.3 presents the accuracy results of our developed approach compared to the aforementioned SOTA algorithms. Table 3.4 showcases the precision scores achieved, while Table 3.5 demonstrates the performance of the evaluated methods in terms of Recall. Finally, Table 3.6 provides a comparison based on F1-score. The best scores for each dataset are highlighted in bold.

TABLE 3.3 – Comparison of the developed approach with six SOTA methods according to the accuracy metric.

ID	Accuracy						
	KNN	MIFW	PM	FKNN	PIFW	ENN	DE4
1	73.7	83.3	83.6	82.2	**84.3**	72.7	79.6
2	53	55.9	55.5	54.5	**56.1**	50.3	51.0
3	95.8	94.5	95.5	95.2	94.5	96.9	**99.3**
4	80.8	79.7	80.8	80.6	**80.9**	66.9	58.4
5	66.0	69.6	**70.8**	65.6	70.1	66.9	69
6	62.4	81.5	81.2	80.7	**84.4**	80	74.4
7	48.2	55.2	**56.0**	49.3	54.7	52.5	53.6
8	82.2	82.1	**86.1**	82.1	83.4	80.7	81.9
9	72.8	76.3	**76.4**	70.9	73.6	72.2	71.5
10	71.1	**75.2**	72.6	73.4	74.8	70.9	71.1
11	70.2	72.5	69.5	71.7	**72.7**	69.2	67.1
12	94.0	94.6	**95.6**	93.8	94.6	92.5	93.3
13	99.3	99.3	98.5	99.2	**99.6**	99.5	99.5
14	84.6	88.3	88.9	86.9	**90.7**	83.2	88.2
15	**92.8**	**92.8**	**92.8**	92.6	**92.8**	92	92.1
16	72.7	75.6	**79.4**	77.4	78.1	73.2	72.4
17	92.3	94.0	93.1	90.8	**94.7**	92.9	91.5
18	80.0	**83.2**	81.6	81.5	82.3	83	80.9
19	**97.2**	83.7	83	90.6	88.5	85.9	87.6
20	54.6	52.3	52.8	**54.8**	55.1	55.5	52.3
21	73.1	77.0	**77.8**	72.8	74.7	73.1	72.5
22	96.0	95.7	94.5	**96.3**	95.9	94.1	94.3
23	76.6	**97.2**	96.8	87.1	92.6	90.7	87.5
24	69.5	58.8	**70.5**	66.2	60.3	65.7	67.3
25	88.8	88.5	88.7	88.1	**88.9**	87.5	87.7
Mean	77.9	80.3	**80.9**	79.4	80.7	77.9	77.8

TABLE 3.4 – Comparison of the developed approach with six SOTA methods according to the precision metric.

ID	Precision						
	KNN	MIFW	PM	FKNN	PIFW	ENN	DE4
1	74.9	82.8	83.3	82.6	**84.8**	72.5	79.9
2	52.9	57.1	56.5	55.5	**57.0**	51.4	52.3
3	96.2	95.0	95.8	95.5	94.8	97.1	**99.3**
4	81.2	80.9	**81.6**	81.2	81.5	67.8	60.3
5	64.9	68.2	**69.9**	64.5	68.7	64.6	67.3
6	62.3	81.9	81.4	80.9	**84.5**	80.6	75.1
7	48.0	54.8	**55.7**	49.1	53.9	52	52.8
8	76.2	80.8	**86.1**	80.9	82.7	80.2	81.3
9	71.0	75.7	**75.9**	71.1	74.0	72.8	72.3
10	71.1	**75.1**	72.5	73.6	74.6	70.7	70.9
11	69.6	**71.7**	68.5	70.6	71.5	68.3	66.4
12	92.6	93.6	**95.2**	92.5	93.6	91.5	93.2
13	99.3	99.3	98.6	99.3	**99.5**	**99.5**	99.4
14	86.3	89.6	89.7	87.3	**90.1**	85.4	89.2
15	**89.3**	**89.3**	**89.3**	89.1	**89.3**	89.0	**89.3**
16	74.5	**76.6**	75.7	73.4	74.1	75.2	73.7
17	90.6	**92.7**	91.4	90.1	92.5	91.6	90.9
18	79.7	**83.2**	81.4	81.1	81.8	82.5	80.3
19	**97.2**	83.6	83.1	90.5	88.6	85.8	87.6
20	**54.8**	52.4	52.9	54.7	55	55.4	52.5
21	69.6	73.2	**74.0**	69.3	70.9	71.5	72.7
22	95.9	95.6	94.4	**96.0**	95.6	93.8	94
23	76.4	**97.3**	96.9	87.2	92.4	90.9	88.8
24	69.7	58.9	**70.5**	66.6	60.1	65.9	67.4
25	**86.7**	86.4	86.6	86	86.3	86.4	85.9
Mean	77.2	79.8	**80.3**	78.7	79.9	77.7	77.7

3.2.3.3 Comparison with other machine learning algorithms

To demonstrate the effectiveness of our method, we conducted a comparative analysis with some of the most widely recognized classification algorithms (as shown in Table 3.7): support vector machine (SVM) (Cortes and Vapnik, 1995), extreme learning machine (ELM) (Huang et al., 2011), stochastic gradient boosting trees (GBDT) (Friedman, 2002), k-Nearest Neighbors (KNN) (Altman, 1992), and Naive Bayes (NB) (Duda and Hart, 2001), as presented in the paper by Zhang et al. (Zhang et al., 2017).

In our experiments, we employed a 10-fold cross-validation approach. Each dataset was divided into three parts. Specifically, 80% of the total examples in each dataset were utilized for training a classification model, another 10% were allocated for parameter tuning, and the remaining 10% were reserved for testing purposes. It's important to note that all classifiers employed the same training and testing examples. We selected ten datasets from the dataset pool used in the study and compared the performance of our method against the algorithms mentioned above.

TABLE 3.5 – Comparison of the developed approach with six SOTA methods according to the Recall metric.

ID	Recall						
	KNN	MIFW	PM	FKNN	PIFW	ENN	DE4
1	73.7	83.3	83.6	82.2	**84.3**	72.7	79.6
2	53.0	55.9	55.5	54.5	**56.1**	50.3	51
3	95.8	94.5	95.5	95.2	94.5	96.9	**99.3**
4	80.8	79.7	80.8	80.6	**80.9**	66.9	58.4
5	66.0	69.6	**70.8**	65.6	70.1	66.9	69
6	61.7	81.1	80.9	**89.8**	82.5	79.2	76.1
7	48.2	55.2	**56.0**	49.3	54.7	52.5	53.6
8	57.1	69.8	**72.7**	68.2	71.4	70.5	61.8
9	61.2	67.8	**68.2**	66.5	68.1	65.3	67.2
10	69.3	**73.8**	71.6	71	72.2	70.3	69.9
11	66.0	67.7	64.8	66.9	**68.1**	65.3	66.4
12	61.8	64.6	**74.4**	73.8	65.9	66.4	63.7
13	99.3	99.3	98.5	99.2	**99.6**	99.5	99.5
14	79.5	84.4	**85.7**	82.7	84.3	85.1	84.4
15	**50.8**	**50.8**	**50.8**	50.7	**50.8**	50.6	**50.8**
16	61.2	**64.5**	60.9	59.6	62	61.4	60.3
17	57.2	**62.7**	59.3	58.9	57.5	59.8	62.4
18	75.6	**79.3**	77.4	77.3	79.1	79.0	76.2
19	**97.1**	83.4	82.9	90.5	88.9	86.1	87.4
20	54.6	52.3	52.8	54.7	55.0	**55.4**	52.6
21	54.8	58.1	**58.6**	54.2	54.1	57.7	56.0
22	**91.2**	90.5	88.5	87.7	89.8	91	89.1
23	72.8	**96.5**	96.1	86.1	90.3	90.1	88.4
24	69.5	58.8	**70.5**	67.2	65.3	65.7	67.3
25	**61.9**	61.3	61.6	60.1	60.9	61.5	57.7
Mean	68.8	72.2	**72.7**	71.7	72.3	70.6	69.9

We conducted a statistical analysis using the STAC platform (Rodríguez-Fdez et al., 2015) to assess the statistical significance of our results. To ascertain whether the differences among these results held statistical significance, we applied a Friedman test to the accuracy outcomes, which are detailed in Table 3.3. Table 3.8 provides an assessment of the statistical significance of the distinctions between our developed approach (PM) and the state-of-the-art techniques.

3.2.3.4 Analysis of the results

From the results presented in Table 3.3, it's evident that our proposed PM method outperforms other techniques on nine out of the twenty-five datasets. Additionally, the differences in accuracy with competitors on the remaining datasets are negligible. Consequently, the PM algorithm achieves a higher average accuracy compared to all other approaches. Focusing on individual datasets, PM significantly outperforms competitors on Hepatitis, Spect, and Madelon datasets, which stand out due to their high number of attributes relative to examples.

TABLE 3.6 – Comparison of the developed approach with six SOTA methods according to the F1-score metric.

ID	F1-score						
	KNN	MIFW	PM	FKNN	PIFW	ENN	DE4
1	77.7	**82.7**	82.6	81.7	82.3	79.1	80.5
2	51.9	55.0	54.7	52.9	**55.8**	51.2	50.7
3	95.8	94.5	95.4	95.3	94.4	96.7	**98.1**
4	80.9	80.2	**81.1**	80.8	**81.1**	68.2	61.3
5	65.1	68.5	**69.9**	68.4	68.8	65.5	68.3
6	62.1	81.4	81.1	80.9	**82.2**	79	76.2
7	47.8	54.8	**55.6**	48.8	53.9	52.1	53.3
8	77.5	81.2	**84.9**	84.7	79.4	80.1	80.2
9	71.6	75.9	**76.1**	74.5	75.1	75.3	74.2
10	70.6	**74.9**	72.5	73	72.2	70.3	69.9
11	69.8	71.8	68.7	66.9	**68.1**	65.3	66.4
12	93.0	93.7	**95.3**	93.8	94.9	91.4	93.7
13	99.3	99.3	98.5	99.2	**99.6**	99.5	99.5
14	83.6	87.7	**88.5**	86.7	86.3	85.1	84.4
15	**90.8**	**90.8**	**90.8**	90.7	**90.8**	90.6	**90.8**
16	73.4	75.8	**76.3**	72.9	75.5	74.6	73.7
17	91.3	**93.0**	92.0	91.7	92.8	**93.0**	91.4
18	79.3	**82.7**	81	80.3	80.9	79.0	76.2
19	**97.2**	83.6	83	90.5	88.9	86.1	87.4
20	54.4	52.2	52.6	54.7	55.0	**55.4**	52.6
21	70.9	73.7	**74.1**	73.2	72.5	71.9	70.8
22	95.9	95.6	94.4	93.3	**96.1**	95.8	95.4
23	75.9	**97.2**	96.8	94.7	95.9	95.5	94.6
24	69.4	58.6	**70.5**	67.2	65.3	65.7	67.3
25	87.3	87	87.2	85.9	86.7	**88.0**	84.5
Mean	77.3	79.7	**80.1**	79.3	79.8	78.2	77.7

TABLE 3.7 – Comparison of the developed approach against different machine learning algorithms

	Accuracy					
Data	GBDT	ELM	SVM	KNN	NB	PM
pima	70.1	66.2	64.9	61.0	**75.3**	70.1
Iono	**91.7**	89.0	80.6	89.0	80.6	89.7
German	**76.0**	71.0	72.0	72.0	76.0	**79.1**
splice	**94.4**	92.5	92.5	77.4	87.1	93.6
newThy	95.5	95.5	**100.0**	95.5	95.5	96.5
spambase	**92.0**	70.9	91.5	68.9	64.1	85.1
phoneme	86.7	88.0	77.5	**89.3**	73.4	84.7
car	**100.0**	94.8	91.9	85.6	78.6	99.3
Wave	85.2	86.4	83.4	79.6	78.8	**86.4**
Sonar	**90.5**	61.9	**90.5**	71.4	76.2	83.2
Avg	**88.2**	81.6	84.5	79.0	78.6	86.8

When examining precision results (Table 3.4), PM outperforms other algorithms on nine out of the twenty-five datasets, with the best results observed

TABLE 3.8 – Friedman Aligned ranks test according to the results of accuracy presented in Table 3.3

Comparison	Statistic	Adjusted p-value	Result
PM vs DE4	3.49297	0.00334	H0 is rejected
PM vs ENN	3.34863	0.00568	H0 is rejected
PM vs FKNN	2.45374	0.00989	H0 is rejected
PM vs KNN	2.22280	0.01836	H0 is rejected
PM vs PIFW	1.83716	0.02573	H0 is rejected
PM vs MIFW	1.63509	0.02931	H0 is rejected

on datasets like sick, credits, and Madelon, which are characterized by a small number of features compared to examples.

In terms of Recall score (Table 3.5), PM consistently performs significantly better than other methods, surpassing competitors on ten out of twenty-five datasets.

Regarding the F1-score (Table 3.6), the PM method achieves the highest value on twelve out of the twenty-five datasets. While the proposed technique performs better than all other methods on two out of the ten datasets in Table 3.7, it maintains competitive accuracy levels on the remaining datasets, except for "Spambase" and "Sonar" where the difference is more substantial. On average, the developed approach achieves higher accuracy compared to SVM, NB, KNN, and ELM but slightly lags behind GBDT.

The statistical analysis in Table 3.8 indicates significant performance differences when comparing PM with DE4, PM with ENN, and PM with FKNN, as evidenced by p-values less than 0.01. This suggests a considerable gap in performance favoring the developed approach.

Based on these results, it is safe to conclude that our suggested approach offers superior classification performance and generalization capabilities compared to other state-of-the-art techniques in this study. This success can be attributed to the following factors:

- PM prioritizes features that appear most frequently in reliable association rules.
- The use of information gain helps cover cases where association rules alone may not yield satisfactory results.

3.2.4 Summary of the chapter

The first study introduced an innovative ensemble method based on the K-nearest neighbors (KNN) algorithm. This approach entails constructing multiple KNN models by employing various bootstrap examples and employing feature selection methods grounded in correlation analysis. The experimental assessment showcased the method's efficiency and accuracy in comparison to the classical KNN algorithm, the Approximate Nearest Neighbor (ANN) algorithm, and the Ensemble Method of KNN (EMKNN), across all three performance metrics.

The developed approach efficiently harnesses a subset of features for each estimator, surpassing other algorithms. This superiority can be attributed to the method's capacity to weed out irrelevant attributes, resulting in significant enhancements in memory usage, execution speed, and overall performance.

As part of our future research direction for the initial paper within this chapter, we have plans to explore the applicability of this feature selection technique in other ensemble methods. Additionally, we aim to investigate its potential as a feature weighting technique and assess its effectiveness when applied to various machine learning algorithms.

In our second study, we introduced an innovative feature weighting approach designed specifically for the kNN algorithm. This method harnesses the combined power of association rules and information gain to fine-tune feature weights. Importantly, our model's feature weights are influenced by the labeling of training points.

We conducted a comprehensive evaluation of our proposed model on 25 real-world datasets characterized by diverse features. In this evaluation, we compared our approach to six state-of-the-art and widely recognized classifiers.

The results obtained from our experiments demonstrate that our developed approach not only operates effectively without requiring additional parameter adjustments but also exhibits a substantial advantage over certain well-established classifiers.

Chapter 4

New Random Forest Pruning Techniques

Contents

In this chapter, we present two innovative Random Forest pruning approaches. The first technique, introduces a novel strategy for forest pruning called PRM, which utilizes association rules metrics. The PRM method functions by initially extracting branches from the initial forest, then calculating a score for each branch using association rules metrics and eliminating those with low scores. Ultimately, it employs the selected branches to generate predictions on unseen data by aggregating their predictions. The second finding introduces a new machine learning algorithm designed to prune Random Forests using naïve Bayes formulas for predicting student performance. This algorithm is applied to two distinct student datasets and is subsequently compared to seven other machine-learning algorithms. The experimental results provide compelling evidence that the new algorithm achieves strong performance.

4.1 Optimizing the number of branches in a decision forest using association rule metrics

4.1.1 Introduction

Ensemble learning approaches offer significant power, yet a notable drawback is their tendency to train excessively large ensembles. These oversized ensembles can be memory-intensive since they require storage for numerous base learners and often result in longer prediction times. Interestingly, rather than enhancing performance, a large ensemble can sometimes hinder generalization. To address these issues, various methods have been developed to enhance classification performance and reduce ensemble size through pruning.

Ensemble pruning techniques focus on identifying a subset of learners capable of accurate predictions on unseen data. Much of the research in this field has centered on ensemble selection, aiming to pinpoint the optimal set of base learners for prediction. Other approaches seek to find an optimal subset of branches within the ensemble instead of entire trees, while some strive to transform the initial forest into a single tree. Additionally, there are alternative methods, such as individual tree pruning, where each tree is pruned independently, and the pruned trees are combined for prediction.

Pruning a forest typically introduces additional computational costs during the training phase, as there is an emphasis on identifying a high-performing sub-forest. However, the reduction in ensemble size can lead to a more manageable and computationally efficient model during implementation and prediction. Forest pruning approaches can be categorized into different types: optimization-based pruning, clustering-based pruning, and sorting-based pruning. The primary objective of forest pruning is to establish an effective metric for evaluating the quality of a specific tree or branch.

Inspired by the utility of association rule metrics in data analysis, we introduce a novel metric for evaluating branches within a Random Forest, based on association rule metrics. This method calculates the importance of each branch using a measure that incorporates support and confidence. Subsequently, it selects the best branches to constitute the final branch set, which is then employed to make predictions for new data.

4.1.2 Motivation

We employed a formula that combines support and confidence measures, recognizing their significance as key factors in the selection of pertinent categorization rules. Moreover, we integrated support as an exponent of confidence, as our observations revealed that confidence holds a more pivotal role than support. In essence, high support signifies the strength of the relationship between items, whereas high confidence reflects a strong dependency between the antecedent and consequent of the rule which represents the target attribute. These measures are pivotal for the identification of applicable categorization rules, a vital aspect of our proposed approach. In summary, we used these two measures since they are often used together to identify meaningful and interesting patterns in large datasets.

4.1.3 PRM pruning method

Our developed approach, PRM (Pruning Random Forest using Association Rules Metrics), adopts a static pruning approach. To begin, PRM constructs the forest and extracts branches from each tree. Subsequently, it computes the score for each branch using support and confidence measures (as defined in Eq. 4.1). Following this, PRM arranges the branches in descending order based on their scores and chooses the top M branches to constitute the final subset. Finally, this selected subset is utilized to classify new instances by aggregating their predictions through a majority vote mechanism.

4.1.3.1 Preliminaries

Definition 1 - Classification Rule or branch: A classification rule represents the path from the root of a tree to a leaf. It has the form of:
"$IFcondition\_1$ AND $condition\_2$ AND ... AND $condition\_N$ THEN $class\_label$".
Where $condition\_1, condition\_2, \ldots,$ and $condition\_N$ are conditions that represent the split attribute and the best threshold present in each node of the branch.
Definition 2 - Branch score: The score of a branch is calculated using the following formula:

$$score(br) = confidence(br)^{(support(br))} \tag{4.1}$$

Where br is the branch, we want to evaluate. $Support(br)$ is the support of the branch, and it is calculated using (Eq. 4.2). $Confidence(br)$ is the branch's confidence, calculated using (Eq. 4.3). A branch is a conditional implication in the form $X => Y$ where X, Y are items. To identify interesting rules in the dataset, there are two key metrics in measuring association rule mining results: the rule's support and confidence.

$$support(br) = \frac{frequency(X,Y)}{N} \tag{4.2}$$

Where $frequency(X, Y)$ is the size of the majority class in the branches leaf node and N is the number of examples in the dataset.

$$confidence(br) = \frac{frequency(X, Y)}{frequencey(X)} \tag{4.3}$$

Where $frequency(X)$ is the number of examples reaching the leaf node in the branch br.

4.1.3.2 Example illustrating the operating process of the PRM algorithm

We've included an example of a decision tree to offer a clearer insight into how our algorithm functions. This illustration aims to simplify the comprehension of the PRM algorithm's operational process. Since we employ an ensemble of trees, we are showcasing the operation of a single tree, and this applies uniformly to the other trees within the forest. The tree depicted in Figure 4.1 is constructed using the playTennis dataset as a demonstration.

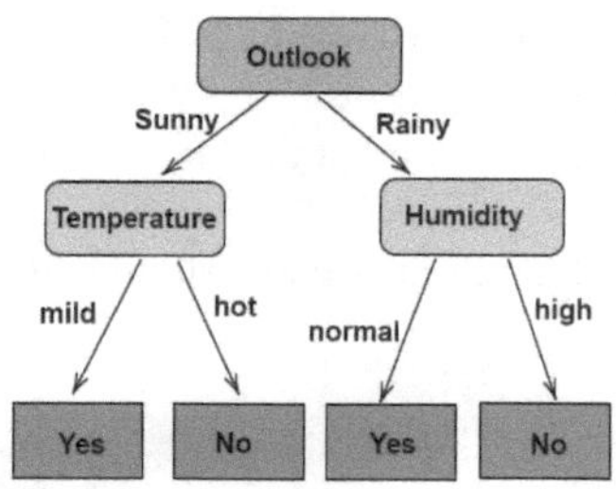

FIGURE 4.1 – Example of a decision tree using the playTennis dataset.

After extracting the rules from the above tree. The rules have the following form:

$(Outlook = Sunny)and(Temperature = mild) => [playTennis = Yes]$
$(Outlook = Sunny)and(Temperature = hot) => [playTennis = No]$
$(Outlook = Rainy)and(Humidity = normal) => [playTennis = Yes]$
$(Outlook = Rainy)and(Humidity = high) => [playTennis = No]$

Next, we calculate the support and confidence of these rules using the following approach:

Consider the rule: "IF Outlook = Sunny AND Temperature = Mild THEN playTennis = Yes."

1. **Support**: If, out of 100 examples in the training dataset, 20 satisfy the conditions of this rule (i.e., they have Outlook = Sunny, Temperature =

Mild, and playTennis = Yes), then the support of the rule is calculated as 20/100, which equals 0.2.

2. **Confidence**: To determine the confidence of the same rule, suppose we have 40 out of 100 examples in the training dataset that have Outlook = Sunny AND Temperature = Mild. Therefore, the confidence is calculated as the proportion of instances that satisfy both the antecedent and consequent of the rule, which is 20/40, equal to 0.5.
3. **Score**: Finally, the score of this branch is computed as the confidence raised to the power of support, resulting in a value of $0.5^{0.2}$, which is approximately equal to 0.87.

These steps provide a more detailed explanation of the proposed method:

- **Step 1.** Create N bootstrap samples from the given training data.
- **Step 2.** Build trees on all the bootstrap samples using the random forest method.
- **Step 3.** Extract branches from the forest.
- **Step 4.** Compute the score for each branch.
- **Step 5.** Rank the branches in ascending order according to their score.
- **Step 6.** Select the best M branches.
- **Step 7.** Aggregate the prediction of the M branches to predict the class of new examples.

An illustrative flowchart of the proposed algorithm is shown in Fig. 4.2.

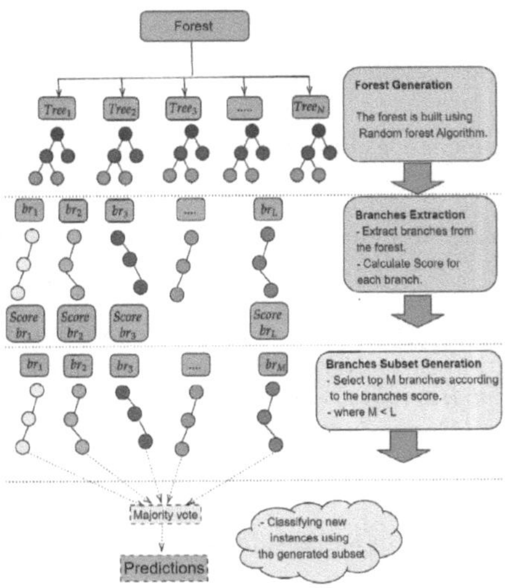

FIGURE 4.2 – Flowchart explaining the principle of the PRM method.

The algorithm's primary objective is to enhance the accuracy of rules by assessing the significance of each connected element within the forest and its relationships with the generated rules. This assessment adheres to the categorization scheme of the Random Forest model. It's important to note that our rule generation process does not prioritize interpretability, as creating interpretable "IF...THEN..." rules from well-structured decision trees within a random forest is straightforward. However, not all of the derived rules are equally valuable.

Furthermore, the original forest might contain redundant or overlapping rules, meaning rules that are similar but provide conflicting predictions. As a result, our algorithm systematically iterates through the rules, determining which ones should be included in the final rule set. It also aims to exclude redundant rules, thereby enhancing the efficiency and effectiveness of the resulting rule set. The following algorithm illustrates in detail the working system of the suggested method:

The novelty of our developed approach lies in two key aspects: the introduction of a novel measure for branch evaluation and the utilization of association rule metrics for assessing random forest branches. As far as our knowledge extends, this study represents the pioneering application of association rule metrics to the task of random forest pruning. This novel approach constitutes a substantial and noteworthy contribution to the field.

4.1.4 Results and discussion

4.1.4.1 Datasets

To evaluate the performance of the developed approach, experiments were conducted on twenty real-world datasets freely available in the UCI repository (Asuncion and Newman, 2007) and Kaggle (Kaggle, n.d.) (Table 4.1). The tasks in all datasets are binary classification tasks. We reported the size, the number of nominal and numeric attributes, and the proportion of cases with minority classes for each dataset.

4.1.4.2 Experiment setting

We have performed two experiments to study the feasibility of the developed approach:

- The first experiment compared PRM with four state-of-the-art-algorithms: Optimal tree ensemble (OTE) (Khan et al., 2020), random forest (RF) (Breiman, 2001), Correlation-based Ensemble Selection (CES) (Daho et al., 2021) and Classification algorithm using branches importance (BrC) (Manzali et al., 2021).
- The second experiment compared PRM with different machine learning algorithms Extreme Learning Machine (ELM) (Huang et al., 2011), Support vector machine (SVM)(Cortes and Vapnik, 1995), k-Nearest Neighbors (KNN) (Keller et al., 1985), Stochastic Gradient Boosting Trees (GBDT) (Friedman, 2002), and Naive Bayes(NB) (Hart et al., 2000) presented in the paper (Zhang et al., 2017).

Algorithm 4.1: The PRM Algorithm

Input: A learning set $S := (x_1; y_1), \ldots, (x_n; y_n)$,
features F, and the number of trees in the forest B;
Output: an ensemble of branches

```
begin
    SelectBranches(S, F, B)
    T = ∅
    P = ∅
    Branches = ∅
    for i = 1 to B do
        t_i = CreateTree(S, F)
        T = T ∪ t_i
    end
    for i = 1 to B do
        br_i = extract branches from t_i
        Branches = Branches ∪ br_i
    end
    for i = 1 to len(Branches) do
        sc_i = calculate the score of each branch br_i using Eq.1
    end
    P = select top M branches from Branches according to sc_i
    return P
    End Function
    CreateTree(S, F)
    S_v = Create a bootstrap sample with replacement from S
    for every node do
        f = a random subset of F
        bestSplit = best split feature using f and S_v
        split S_v using bestSplit
    end
    return the learned tree
    End Function
end
```

TABLE 4.1 – Datasets descriptions

#	Dataset	Instances	Features		Classes
			Num	Nom	
1	bands	540	24	15	42.22
2	sonar	208	60	0	46.63
3	eighthr	2533	73	0	6,32
4	clean	6598	166	0	0
5	spambase	4601	57	0	39.40
6	ionosphere	351	34	0	35.9
7	Ds1.100	26733	101	0	3.03
8	adult	32561	6	8	24,08
9	ad	3263	1556	0	13.88
10	caravan	5822	85	0	5.98
11	hill_valley	606	100	0	49,67
12	Connect2	67557	0	42	65.83
13	eye	14980	14	0	44,88
14	bank	41190	10	10	11,27
15	Travel insurance	63326	3	6	1.46
16	Magic04	19020	10	0	35.16
17	titanic	891	15	0	38.38
18	madelon	2000	500	0	50
19	wdbc	569	30	0	37.26
20	pima	768	8	0	0

4.1.4.3 Experimental results

The results have been obtained through a five-fold cross-validation process for each dataset. In our experiment, we've generated 100 trees from each training dataset, resulting in a total of 500 trees. These trees are then assessed for their performance using the respective test datasets. Regarding the parameters, we have employed two specific parameters:

- **maxDepth:** The maximum depth of the tree, maxDepth is varied in the interval[3,9]
- **minSamplesLeaf:** the minimum number of samples required to be at a leaf node. In our experiments minSamplesLeaf takes two values (1,10)

We have chosen two performance metrics, namely Accuracy (Acc) and the area under the ROC curve (AUC), to evaluate the performance of our models. In the first experiment, the reported results represent the average values obtained from the five test datasets, with the best results highlighted in bold. Table 4.2 displays the results for the accuracy and AUC metrics, while Table 4.3 provides information on the number of branches and execution times (in seconds) for the five algorithms, all executed on the same hardware configuration.

TABLE 4.2 – Performance of the developed approach vs. other state-of-the-art methods in terms of accuracy and AUC metrics.

#	Accuracy results					AUC results				
	OTE	CES	BrC	RF	PRM	OTE	CES	BrC	RF	PRM
1	81.5	79.1	82.0	81.5	**83.7**	91.5	92.8	91.3	**94.3**	92.2
2	**86.5**	84.2	83.7	84.2	84.1	91.0	**92.9**	91.4	91.2	91.6
3	**94.2**	93.6	93.8	94.0	94.1	88.4	89.3	**92.5**	90.8	91.0
4	**98.1**	95.2	95.8	97.0	980	98.4	99.0	97.6	**99.1**	98.8
5	94.9	94.1	93.9	94.7	**95.5**	97.9	97.7	92.5	98.4	**98.5**
6	**94.3**	94.2	94.0	**94.3**	93.5	**98.1**	97.5	97.2	97.7	98.0
7	97.3	97.7	98.0	98.0	**98.1**	92.1	91.5	90.3	**92.8**	92.6
8	84.8	85.2	83.7	**85.3**	84.1	84.8	86.0	90.2	90.3	**90.7**
9	94.2	92.9	95.1	94.2	**96.7**	**96.2**	95.0	93.4	**96.2**	95.6
10	**94.0**	93.7	93.8	**94.0**	**94.0**	**76.9**	76.1	75.7	76.5	76.2
11	57.4	57.4	57.0	54.0	**57.7**	58.4	57.2	57.2	55.7	**59.6**
12	75.5	74.1	**80.5**	73.9	80.3	86.5	88.3	87.1	85.4	**89.2**
13	89.7	88.9	84.7	83.9	**88.0**	92.7	91.3	90.1	92.7	**95.2**
14	90.5	89.9	**90.7**	90.6	90.6	**90.5**	89.7	84.9	85.1	85.1
15	98.5	98.5	98.5	98.5	98.5	83.2	**83.6**	83.3	83.1	82.5
16	84.9	85.4	85.3	86.5	**86.7**	90.1	92.0	90.0	92.4	**92.9**
17	83.3	**83.9**	82.7	82.8	82.5	83.3	83.0	84.9	87.0	**87.3**
18	65.8	66.6	**72.0**	69.0	69.5	62.8	53.6	83.2	**76.5**	**76.5**
19	96.8	97.0	95.8	96.5	**97.5**	96.8	97.0	95.6	99.3	**99.4**
20	77.3	77.0	76.2	77.2	**77.6**	81.0	**83.9**	80.8	83.6	83.5
Avg	86.98	86.43	86.86	86.51	**87.54**	87.03	86.87	87.46	88.41	**88.82**

To assess the significance of the previously presented results, we conducted non-parametric statistical tests using the Friedman test along with Finner's posthoc test, employing a significance level of 0.05. We utilized the STAC platform for this analysis Rodríguez-Fdez et al. (2015). Table 4.5 provides the ranking of the methods, while Table 4.6 displays the rank of the algorithms based on the accuracy results presented in Table 4.2.

Table 4.5 clearly demonstrates that the PRM algorithm attains the highest ranking when compared to other state-of-the-art methods. Table 4.6 provides further insight, indicating that all comparisons result in a p-value less than 0.05. This implies a significant difference in performance when compared to PRM for all methods, except in the case of the OTE method, where the p-value exceeds 0.1. This suggests that the distinction between PRM and OTE is too minimal to be deemed statistically significant.

Moving forward, Table 4.7 presents the ranking of the methods, while Table 4.8 outlines the rank of the algorithms based on the accuracy results presented in Table 4.4.

Based on Table 4.7, it's evident that PRM secures the highest rank according to the accuracy score, with GBDT and ELM following closely. Table 4.8 provides additional statistical insights, revealing that the adjusted p-values for the first three comparisons are below the significance level of 0.1. This

TABLE 4.3 – Comparison of the developed approach with other state-of-the-art methods according to two aspects: the number of branches and the execution time.

#	Forest size (number of branches)					Run time in sec				
	OTE	CES	BrC	RF	PRM	OTE	CES	BrC	RF	PRM
1	**1925**	2342	2599	3209	2246	22.5	31.4	**17.2**	37.6	30.8
2	1186	1130	**628**	1396	823	29.1	34.1	25.7	40.9	**22.3**
3	5504	4953	**3975**	6116	5076	35.8	**34.4**	35	73.6	38.9
4	6833	6235	**4441**	8542	7089	81.9	88.3	**73.6**	109.2	78.8
5	6056	6315	**3893**	8652	7786	101.7	115.4	**36.3**	92.8	98.6
6	467	490	**379**	584	484	17.1	21.8	18.5	**16.3**	20.3
7	6440	7486	**4910**	8050	5232	309.8	364.5	**181.4**	498.1	264.3
8	9839	10166	**7105**	10932	9292	189.6	188.2	**107**	211.2	161.3
9	1626	1881	1626	2323	**1370**	654	619	**205.3**	991.3	548.9
10	1714	1787	**1102**	2449	1518	88.4	92.2	**41**	88.7	86.5
11	1622	1237	1318	2028	**1196**	165.8	136.2	**62.4**	144	141.7
12	24608	21839	**20762**	30760	21532	687	711.8	**253**	1376.6	624.8
13	14487	14004	11267	16097	**9980**	59.1	53.9	**35**	61.9	55.9
14	11909	12306	**7542**	13233	10586	194.4	179.8	**62.5**	317.1	184.3
15	13722	**9605**	9777	17153	11149	228.1	204.3	**189.7**	245.5	216.3
16	12912	16048	**7378**	18446	15310	99.7	**81.4**	88.6	95.3	84.2
17	6327	7355	**4824**	7909	6089	31.6	41.4	49.5	37.1	**33.7**
18	5818	5662	**3490**	7757	5042	325.6	298.1	**175.6**	642.2	267.1
19	976	911	**569**	1627	1220	22.8	**17**	21.9	43	26.8
20	1590	1907	1839	2271	**1476**	11.5	10.2	**6.3**	15.7	9.8
Avg	6778.1	6682.9	**4971.2**	8476.7	6224.8	167.78	166.17	**84.28**	266.55	149.77

TABLE 4.4 – Comparison of the PRM algorithm with different classification algorithms in terms of accuracy.

dataset	GBDT	ELM	SVM	KNN	NB	PRM
pima	70.1	66.2	64.9	61.0	**75.3**	71.4
iono	91.7	88.9	80.6	88.9	80.6	**92.9**
German	**76.0**	71.0	72.0	72.0	**76.0**	75.9
splice	**94.4**	92.5	92.5	77.4	87.2	93.2
thyroid	95.5	95.5	**100.0**	95.5	95.4	99.1
spam	**91.9**	70.9	91.5	68.9	64.1	88.7
phoneme	86.7	88.0	77.5	**89.3**	73.4	88.0
car	**100.0**	94.8	91.9	85.6	78.6	93.6
wave	85.2	**86.4**	83.4	79.6	78.8	84.3
sonar	90.5	61.9	90.5	71.4	76.2	**92.0**
avg	**88.19**	81.6	84.47	78.96	78.56	87.91

TABLE 4.5 – The ranks of the algorithms according to the results of accuracy in Table 4.2

Algorithms	PRM	OTE	RF	BrC	CES
Rank	68.0	54.6	46.25	43.525	40.125

TABLE 4.6 – Friedman test (significance level of 0.05)

Comparison	Statistic	Adjusted p-value	Result
PRM vs CES	3.03840	0.00948	H_0 is rejected
PRM vs BrC	2.66780	0.01521	H_0 is rejected
PRM vs RF	2.37077	0.02360	H_0 is rejected
PRM vs OTE	1.46061	0.14412	H_0 is accepted

TABLE 4.7 – The ranks of the algorithms presented in Table 4.4

Alg	PRM	GBDT	SVM	ELM	KNN	NB
Rank	43.8	43.45	31.4	28.05	18.25	18.05

indicates that the null hypotheses corresponding to these comparisons were rejected, signifying a significant difference in scores between PRM and these three methods.

However, for the remaining methods, the adjusted p-values exceed 0.1. This suggests that the differences in scores between PRM and these methods can be considered negligible or not statistically significant.

4.1.5 Analysis of the results

According to the results in Table 4.2, PRM demonstrates superior performance compared to other approaches on eight out of the twenty datasets. However, the largest differences between PRM and the other approaches exist in the Sonar, Eye, Titanic, and Madelon datasets. This can be attributed to these datasets having a substantial number of relevant branches in the forest, and removing some branches might have a detrimental impact on the overall ensemble performance. Nevertheless, on average, our developed approach exhibits higher accuracy than the other approaches.

Table 4.2 also reveals that PRM outperforms other approaches in terms of AUC on nine out of the twenty datasets. Similarly, the differences in performance between PRM and the other methods on the remaining datasets are generally small, with notable exceptions like the bank and Madelon datasets. In fact, the average AUC score of PRM surpasses the average AUC obtained by all other methods.

Delving into individual datasets, we observe that the PRM algorithm significantly outperforms its competitors on the Eye and Connect datasets, which have a relatively small number of attributes compared to instances and maintain a balanced class distribution. These results can be attributed to the fact that the branches generated by these datasets largely contain the same subset of features, enabling the PRM algorithm to select frequent and relevant branches effectively.

Regarding the complexity of the forest (Table 4.3), it's evident that BrC generates the smallest-sized model, followed by PRM. In contrast, the remaining methods produce forests of approximately the same size. This outcome

TABLE 4.8 – Post-Hoc comparison for α =0,1 (FRIEDMAN)

Comparison	Statistic	Adjusted p-value	Result
PRM vs NB	3.29695	0.00488	H_0 is rejected
PRM vs KNN	3.27134	0.00488	H_0 is rejected
PRM vs SVM	2.01658	0.07183	H_0 is rejected
PRM vs ELM	1.58766	0.13842	H_0 is accepted
PRM vs GBDT	0.04481	0.96426	H_0 is accepted

is expected since BrC generates a small subset of branches equivalent to a single tree.

In addition to classification performance, execution time is another crucial consideration, particularly for large datasets. Regarding computation time (Table 4.3), it's natural for BrC to be the fastest method since it predicts each new example using a single branch rather than a majority vote. PRM, on the other hand, outperforms the other approaches in terms of computation time for all datasets because the number of branches generated by PRM is substantially lower than that produced by the other methods.

Table 4.4 indicates that PRM outperforms all other techniques on two out of the ten datasets. However, the difference in score from the best method on the remaining datasets is minimal, except for the "Car" dataset. Consequently, our developed approach achieves a higher average accuracy than the SVM, NB, KNN, and ELM methods while slightly trailing behind the GBDT approach.

In summary, the results suggest that PRM utilizes computer resources efficiently, striking the best balance between performance, forest size, and execution time.

4.2 Prediction of student performance using random forest combined with naïve Bayes

4.2.1 Introduction

In today's era, there is a substantial body of research and investigation dedicated to the prediction of students' behavior and related aspects within the field of education (Rastrollo-Guerrero et al., 2020). This increasing interest underscores the acknowledgment of the significance of comprehending and anticipating how students behave in diverse educational contexts. Scholars are delving into a wide range of dimensions, encompassing learning patterns, academic performance, engagement levels, as well as social and emotional well-being. Through these explorations, educators and researchers aspire to gain deeper insights into the dynamics of student behavior, enhance teaching methodologies, and create targeted interventions to favor comprehensive student development. The persistent quest for knowledge in forecasting students' behavior underscores the commitment to enhancing the educational experience and nurturing student achievement (Namoun and Alshanqiti, 2020).

The primary research gap in predicting student performance using machine learning algorithms lies in the limited interpretability and explainability of these models (Alamri and Alharbi, 2021). While machine learning algorithms have exhibited significant potential in accurately predicting student outcomes, they often function as black boxes, rendering it challenging to understand the underlying reasons for their predictions. This lack of interpretability poses a substantial challenge for educators and stakeholders who require actionable insights to effectively support students. The absence of interpretable models for predicting student performance has instigated the objectives of our research.

Hence, this study introduces RFCNB, an innovative machine-learning algorithm that combines Random Forest and Naive Bayes. RFCNB extracts branches from a constructed random forest and subsequently filters them based on the Naive Bayes formula, retaining only the most pertinent branches. The final RFCNB model comprises a limited number of branches, as the prediction process prioritizes importance rankings instead of relying on majority voting.

4.2.2 developed approach

Our proposed classification method entails several key steps. First, we create N random trees, drawing inspiration from the concept of a random forest. Next, we extract branches from these trees and assess their quality using the Naive Bayes formula. Subsequently, we filter out inferior branches. Ultimately, we utilize the selected branches to make predictions on unseen data by aggregating their individual predictions. The primary steps of our developed approach are illustrated in the following flowchart (Figure 4.3). To evaluate the importance of each branch, we calculate a score for each one using Equation (4.4). This score acts as a measure of importance in the classification procedure.

In the classification phase, we start by arranging the branches in descending order based on their importance scores. Then, we classify instances from the test set using these branches. We begin by selecting the branch with the highest importance and use it to classify unseen examples. Afterward, we proceed with the next branch in the order of importance and classify the remaining examples. This process continues until all examples in the test set have been classified.

Our goal in selecting branches based on their importance and using them for classification is to enhance the accuracy and efficiency of the classification process in our developed approach.

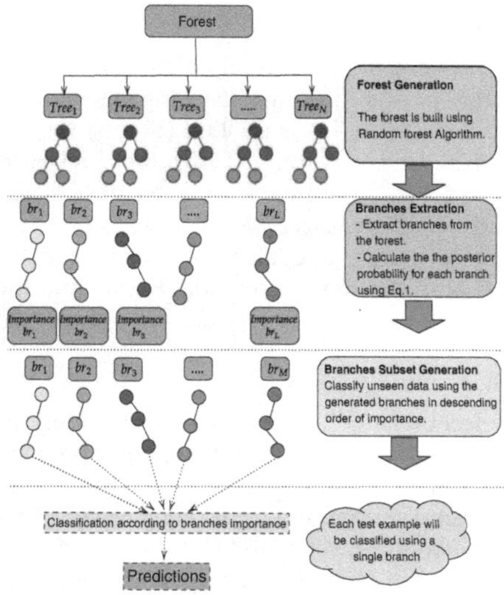

FIGURE 4.3 – Flowchart of the RFCNB method.

4.2.2.1 branch importance

The determination of a branch's importance relies on the probabilities associated with examples reaching the leaf node starting from the root. To quantify the significance of a branch, we employ the posterior probability of Naïve Bayes. This particular probability is computed using the following formula:

$$P(y \mid x_1, x_2, ..., x_n) = P(x_1, x_2, ..., x_n \mid y) \times P(y)/P(x_1, x_2, ..., x_n) \quad (4.4)$$

Each branch of the tree can be considered as an implication expression of the form of $x_1, x_2, ..., x_n \rightarrow y$ where $x_1, x_2, ..., x_n$ is an ensemble of split conditions, and y is the outcome of this branch. Each split condition x_i represents a node in the branch. $P(y)$ is the prior probability of class y, representing the probability of encountering class y in the dataset.

$P(x_1, x_2, ..., x_n \mid y)$ is the conditional probability of features $x_1, x_2, ..., x_n$ given class y. It represents the probability of observing feature $x_1, x_2, \ldots, x_n$ when the class is y.

$P(x_1, x_2, ..., x_n)$ is the evidence or marginal probability of observing the features $x_1, x_2, ..., x_n$.

$P(y \mid x_1, x_2, ..., x_n)$ is the posterior probability of class y given the features $x_1, x_2, ..., x_n$. This is the probability we want to calculate.

4.2.3 Experimantal results

To assess the effectiveness of the RFCNB algorithm, we conducted a comparison with seven other popular machine learning algorithms: Logistic Regression (Hosmer Jr et al., 2013), Decision Tree (Breiman et al., 1984), Support Vector Machine (Cortes and Vapnik, 1995), Random Forest (Breiman, 2001), Adaboost (Freund and Schapire, 1997), K-Nearest Neighbors (Cover and Hart, 1967b), and Gaussian Naïve Bayes (Dempster et al., 1977). The performance of these algorithms was evaluated using four distinct metrics to measure their effectiveness: Accuracy, Precision, Recall, and the AUC (Area Under the ROC Curve).

4.2.3.1 Compared Algorithms

We have chosen a selection of well-established and widely-used machine learning algorithms to compare with our developed approach. These algorithms encompass a variety of techniques tailored for classification tasks, each with its own distinct strengths and underlying assumptions. The selection of the most suitable algorithm depends on the specific problem under consideration and the unique characteristics of the dataset being analyzed. Through the evaluation and comparison of our developed approach with these established algorithms, our objective is to gain a deeper understanding of its performance and determine how competitive it is in addressing the given problem.

- **Logistic Regression (LR)** (Hosmer Jr et al., 2013): A statistical algorithm used for binary or multi-class classification. It models the relationship between a set of independent variables and a binary or categorical dependent variable, using the logistic function to estimate the probability of the outcome.
- **Decision Tree (DT)** (Breiman et al., 1984): A tree-like model that makes decisions based on a series of if-else conditions. It splits the data based on features to create a tree structure, allowing for classification or regression by traversing the tree from root to leaf.
- **Support Vector Machine (SVM)** (Cortes and Vapnik, 1995): A supervised learning algorithm that separates data points into different classes by finding an optimal hyperplane in a high-dimensional space. It aims to maximize the margin between different classes and can handle both linear and non-linear classification tasks.
- **Random Forest (RF)** (Breiman, 2001): An ensemble learning method that constructs multiple decision trees and combines their predictions. It randomly selects subsets of features and data samples to build each tree, reducing overfitting and improving accuracy and robustness.
- **Adaboost (Adaptive Boosting) (AdB)** (Freund and Schapire, 1997): An ensemble learning technique that combines weak learners, typically decision trees, to create a strong learner. It assigns higher weights to misclassified instances in each iteration, focusing on difficult cases and gradually improving overall performance.

- **K-Nearest Neighbors (KNN)** (Cover and Hart, 1967b): A non-parametric algorithm that classifies instances based on their similarity to the k nearest neighbors in the feature space. It assigns a class label based on majority voting among the nearest neighbors.
- **Gaussian Naïve Bayes (GNB)** (Dempster et al., 1977): A probabilistic algorithm based on Bayes' theorem that assumes feature independence. It calculates the probability of a class given the features by estimating the conditional probabilities of each feature, making it efficient and widely used for classification tasks.

4.2.3.2 Used hyper-parameters

The main parameters used for each of the algorithms, along with their typical range of values, are listed below. These parameters were obtained using the grid search method.

TABLE 4.9 – Algorithm parameters

Method	Params	Values range
Logistic Regression	Regularization parameter (C)	from 1 to 10.
	Penalty type Either	L1 (Lasso) or L2 (Ridge)
	Maximum number of iterations	Set to 100
Decision tree	Maximum depth	3 to 9
	Min Sample Leaf	1,10
Support Vector Machine	Kernel type	linear, polynomial, RBF
	Kernel coefficient (gamma)	from 0.001 to 10
Random Forest	The number of trees	100
	Maximum depth	3 to 9
	Min Sample Leaf	1,10
Adaboost	Number of estimators	100
	Learning rate	0.01 to 10
	Base estimator	Decision tree
KNN	Number of neighbors	3,5,7
Gaussian Naïve Bayes	var smoothing	0.1 to 1
RFCNB	The number of trees	100
	Maximum depth	3 to 9
	Min Sample Leaf	1,10

4.2.3.3 Results

To obtain the results we reported, we utilized a five-fold cross-validation methodology. We divided the dataset into five distinct subsets or folds. During each iteration of the process, four of these folds were employed for training or model fitting, while the remaining fold was set aside for testing or evaluating the model's performance. Consequently, the presented results represent the average performance across these five folds. The use of cross-validation serves to mitigate potential biases and offers a more dependable estimate of the model's performance by incorporating multiple subsets of the data for both training and testing. This approach enables a more robust assessment of the algorithm's effectiveness and its ability to generalize to unseen data.

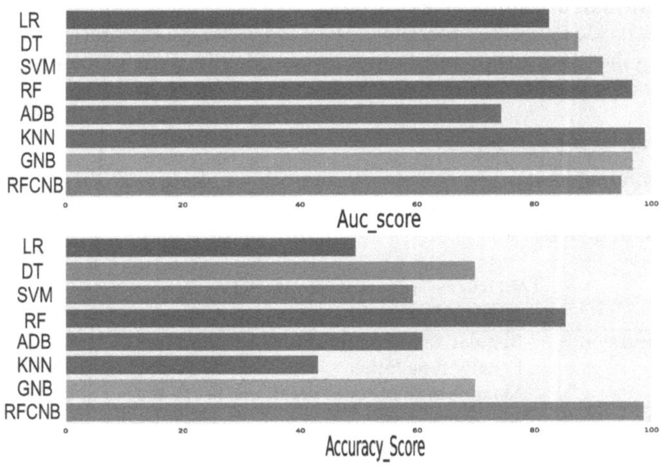

FIGURE 4.4 – Comparison of the methods using accuracy and AUC metrics for the first dataset (student.por).

4.2.3.3.1 Results using the first dataset (student.por) Figures 4.4 and 4.5 display the comparison of the developed approach against the seven compared methods using the first dataset, based on four performance metrics. Meanwhile, Figure 4.6 illustrates the same comparison in terms of execution time.

4.2.3.3.2 Results using the second dataset (student.mat) The comparison of the developed approach against the seven compared methods using the second dataset is depicted in Figures 4.7 and 4.8, showcasing the evaluation based on four performance metrics. Figure 4.9, on the other hand, illustrates the comparison regarding execution time.

4.2.4 Results analysis

Based on the results obtained from the first dataset (student.por), it's evident that our developed approach outperforms its competitors significantly across three key performance metrics: accuracy, precision, and recall. However, when considering the AUC metric, RFCNB ranks fourth, trailing behind RF, KNN, and GNB. It's important to note, though, that the performance gap between RFCNB and the top-performing model is not significantly substantial.

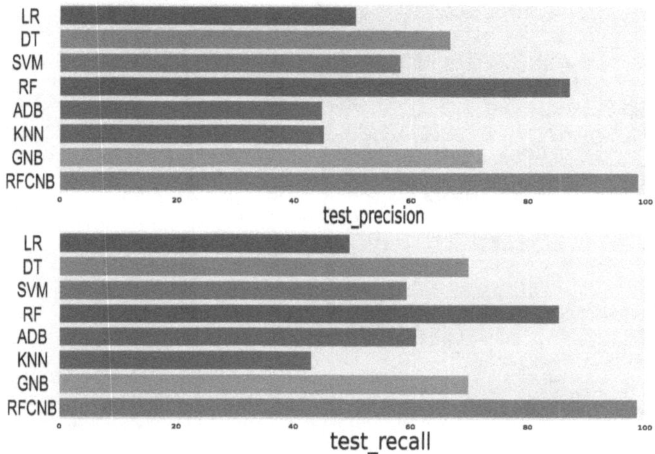

FIGURE 4.5 – Comparison of the methods using precision and Recall metrics for the first dataset (student.por).

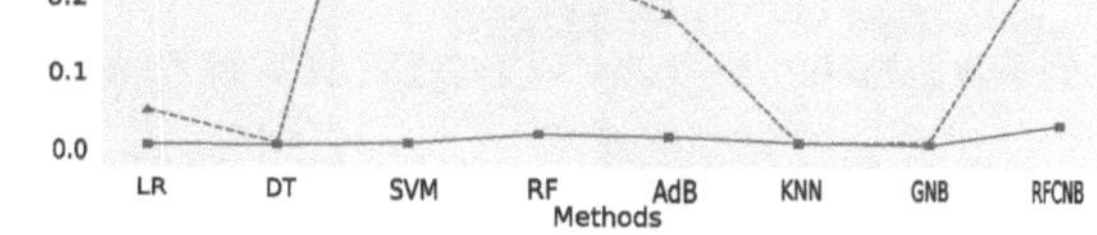

FIGURE 4.6 – Comparison of the methods according to the execution time for the first dataset (student.por).

Shifting our focus to the results of the second dataset (student.mat), the performance of our developed approach remains consistent with what we observed in the first dataset. It maintains its fourth-place ranking in terms of AUC while surpassing its competitors in other metrics. RF secures the second position in this ranking, followed by DT and GNB.

Regarding execution time, most methods exhibit similar prediction times. However, there is a noticeable difference in training time, with SVM, RF, AdB, and RFCNB requiring a longer duration to build their models. Upon

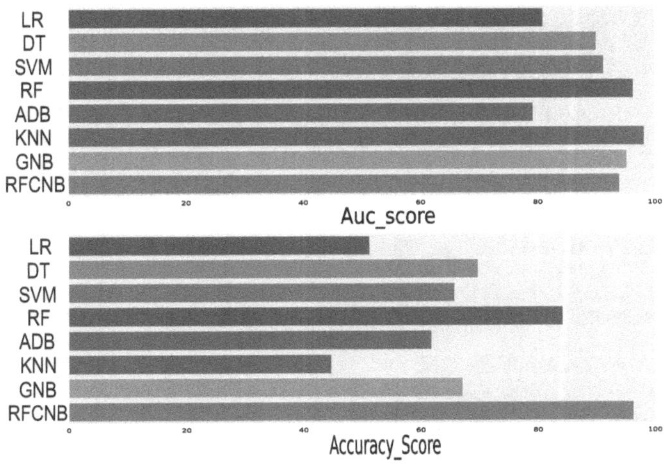

FIGURE 4.7 – Comparison of the methods using accuracy and AUC metrics for the second dataset (student.mat).

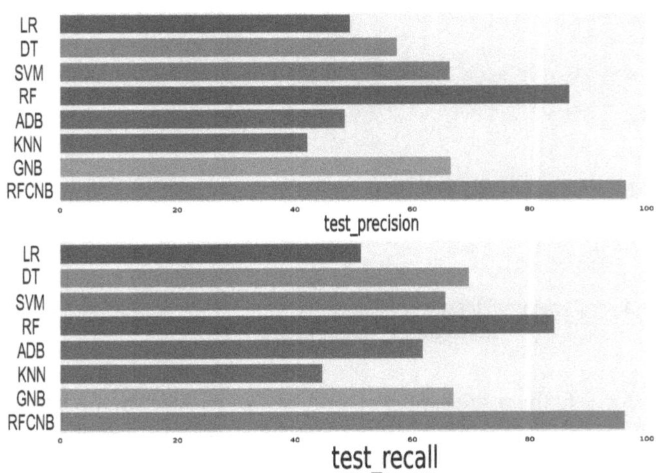

FIGURE 4.8 – Comparison of the methods using precision and Recall metrics for the second dataset (student.mat).

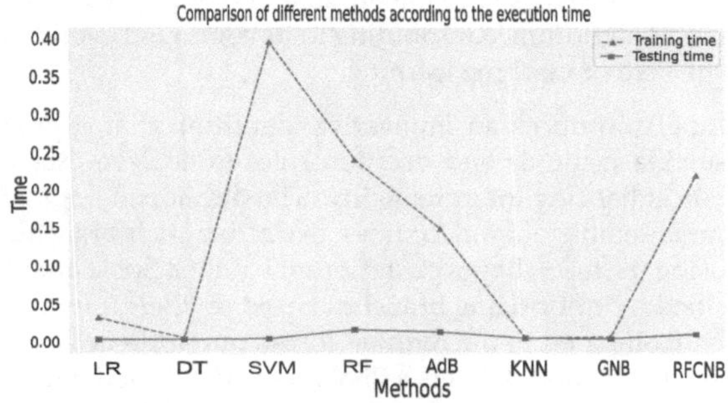

FIGURE 4.9 – Comparison of the methods according to the execution time for the second dataset (student.mat).

closer analysis of the results, it becomes apparent that RFCNB efficiently utilizes available computing resources, offering a favorable balance between performance and execution time. Moreover, its model's interpretability makes RFCNB an effective method for analyzing school data.

4.3 Summary of the chapter

Ensemble methods are widely acclaimed in the realm of machine learning for their superior performance. However, they do come under scrutiny for their substantial memory requirements, extended execution times, and a perceived lack of contribution from all members in the final prediction. Consequently, numerous research endeavors have focused on reducing ensemble size while preserving or even improving performance. In this context, we have introduced in the first finding a method called PRM, a novel forest pruning technique that uses association rule metrics. PRM evaluates the branches within the initial forest using a criterion grounded in support and confidence metrics. It subsequently organizes and selects an optimized subset for making predictions on new data by aggregating their individual predictions.

Our experimental results, covering 20 benchmark datasets, affirm that PRM effectively reduces forest size while elevating overall performance. When compared to alternative forest pruning methods, our results underscore PRM's efficiency in terms of performance, computational time, and forest size.

Nonetheless, despite these promising results, there remain several avenues for future exploration, including:

- Test our developed approach on larger and multiclass datasets.
- The use of other criteria to select the optimal subset of branches.
- Apply the PRM algorithm to different ensemble methods.

These directions for future work hold the promise of refining and expanding the utility of the PRM algorithm, contributing to its continued evolution and applicability in the field of machine learning.

The second finding introduces an innovative algorithm that exploits the strengths of ensemble methods and decision rules to achieve exceptional performance while enhancing interpretability. The developed approach involves creating an ensemble of random trees, extracting their branches, and assessing them using the naive Bayes posterior probability. Subsequently, instances are classified by prioritizing branches based on their importance in descending order. Compared to the random forest, our approach generates branches of higher quality and delivers a final model that is both more interpretable and faster during the prediction phase. In the evaluation conducted on two student performance datasets, our developed approach outperforms all other algorithms across three key performance metrics. These results underscore the efficacy of our approach and encourage fellow researchers to explore the techniques employed in this study for addressing relevant problems. As part of our future work, we plan to assess new eXplainable AI (XAI) libraries and datasets from the realm of education, enabling the generation of diverse local and global explanations. Furthermore, we believe that conducting additional comparative studies may lead to the identification of novel research avenues.

Chapter 5

A New Clustering Method Using Frequent Item Sets

Contents

This chapter introduces an innovative approach to clustering based on frequencies, utilizing frequent item sets as its foundation. This novel technique marks the emergence of a distinct avenue in search methodology, shifting away from conventional distance-based approaches. Our proposed clustering algorithm consists of three primary phases. Initially, we create frequent item sets. Subsequently, we construct cluster centroids using a novel metric called Fi-distance, which combines Euclidean distance with a similarity measure designed for item sets. Finally, each item is assigned to its appropriate cluster based on its degree of membership. When tested on various datasets, including both synthetic and real data, our new method exhibits superior performance compared to existing State-Of-The-Art algorithms.

5.1 Introduction

Clustering is a fundamental data analysis technique that involves categorizing data based on certain criteria, grouping similar samples together while ensuring dissimilarity with samples in other categories. This method finds applications across various fields, including recommender systems, pattern recognition, social network analysis, bioinformatics, data mining, and image processing.

Unsupervised learning encompasses clustering, as it entails organizing data without knowledge of class labels. Clustering approaches aim to optimize a global objective function, often influenced by parameters such as model similarity. The clustering problem is tackled by grouping data points into clusters, with the quality of results evaluated using the objective function.

Statistically, clustering techniques can be broadly classified into nonparametric and probabilistic model-based methods. The latter, including the mixture likelihood technique, assumes that data points follow a mixed probability model. The expectation and maximization technique (EM) is commonly employed in model-based clustering.

Nonparametric methods for clustering can be categorized into partitional and hierarchical techniques, with partitional methods being more prevalent. These techniques rely on an objective function based on similarity or dissimilarity metrics. Data objects are iteratively redistributed across clusters to minimize the objective function until a stopping condition is met.

The k-means algorithm is a widely used partitioning-based clustering method due to its speed and simplicity. It involves two iterative phases: initializing 'k' cluster centers, either randomly or through optimization algorithms, and assigning data objects to clusters based on proximity to the nearest center. Cluster centers are updated by recalculating the mean of data objects in each cluster, and this process continues until convergence.

The choice of a suitable dissimilarity measure is crucial for the effectiveness of clustering algorithms. Euclidean distance is a common measure but is suitable only for linear cluster boundaries. Pattern-based clustering algorithms, on the other hand, group data points based on patterns or features. These algorithms maximize similarity within clusters while minimizing similarity between different clusters, using patterns to capture shared attributes or characteristics among data points.

In this work, we propose a novel clustering approach based on frequency. It begins by generating frequent elements using the FP-growth algorithm and selecting 'k' centers to maximize the dissimilarity between them using a new measure called the FI-distance. This measure combines the Euclidean distance with item set similarity, providing a unique perspective for clustering analysis.

5.2 Developed approach

5.2.1 Motivation

Applying frequent itemsets within the context of clustering can yield numerous advantages and valuable insights. However, it's important to acknowledge that the effectiveness of this approach can be contingent on the particular context and the dataset under consideration. Here, we present various justifications, rationales, and evaluations for incorporating frequent itemsets into the clustering process:

- **Discovering complex patterns**: Frequent item sets highlight widespread co-occurrences or connections between items in a data set. In the field of clustering, these connections provide a valuable tool for revealing hidden relationships between data points, which may not be easily discernible by relying solely on conventional distance measurements.
- **Enhanced Feature Representation**: The presence of frequent itemsets can provide an enriched representation of data points. This can be particularly useful in cases where certain combinations of attributes are more indicative of cluster membership than individual attributes themselves.
- **Dimensionality Reduction**: Concentrating on frequent itemsets offers an effective means of reducing dataset dimensionality. This approach simplifies the clustering procedure and has the potential to enhance clustering performance, particularly when confronted with high-dimensional datasets.
- **Noise Robustness**: Integrating frequent itemsets can make clustering algorithms more resilient against noise and outliers. Because frequent itemsets rely on recurring patterns in the data, they are more resilient to isolated instances of noise.
- **Preprocessing for Other Algorithms**: Frequent itemsets can function as a preliminary step for other clustering algorithms. By pinpointing pertinent attribute combinations, you have the potential to enhance the efficacy of subsequent clustering methodologies.

5.2.2 Methodology Overview

We introduce CFI, a novel clustering approach utilizing Frequent Itemsets (FIs), which are essentially collections or groups of items treated as unified entities. CFI takes a frequency-based research approach as opposed to utilizing distance metrics. Our inspiration derives from the insight that generating frequent item sets with strong support implies a commonality of characteristics among the records linked to that particular item set. The subsequent diagram (Fig 5.1) succinctly outlines the key phases of our developed approachology.

CFI's process commences by employing the FP-growth algorithm (Han et al., 2000) to generate frequent item sets. These sets are then refined by eliminating subsets and single-item sets. Following this refinement, CFI proceeds to determine centroids as follows:

1. **Initial Centroid Selection**: In the initial iteration, CFI designates the item set with the highest support as the centroid of the first cluster.

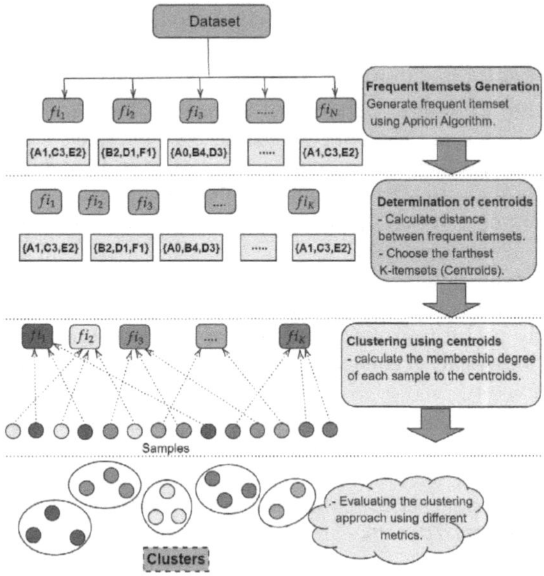

FIGURE 5.1 – Flowchart showing the main phases of the developed approach.

2. **Iterative Centroid Assignment**: Depending on the desired number of clusters, CFI iterates through the remaining item sets in ascending order of support. For each iteration, it calculates the FI-distance between the centroid of the first cluster and all the other remaining frequent item sets. The frequent item set with the maximum distance from this centroid becomes the centroid of the second cluster. This iterative process continues until centroids are established for all requested clusters.

Once these clusters are formed, they are used to group the data using a metric known as the degree of membership. This metric assigns each data item to the nearest centroid. It's important to note that all the item sets in this process are categorical. When dealing with numerical values, a preprocessing step is employed. This step involves transforming numerical values into intervals, which are subsequently further refined into categories. To accomplish this, the binning method (Han et al., 2012) is utilized for interval conversion. The chosen discretization technique is Equal-Frequency Discretization, ensuring that each interval holds an equal number of examples after the transformation.

5.2.3 The FI-distance

Definition 1: (Euclidean Distance).
The Euclidean distance, represented as D_E, is typically a measure of the

straight-line distance between two data samples. However, in this context, we will employ it to calculate the distance between two item sets. This calculation is performed using Equation 5.1.

$$D_E(A,B) = \sqrt{\sum_{i=1}^{i=n} (A_i - B_i)^2} \tag{5.1}$$

Where:
A_i is the presence (1) or absence (0) of the $i-th$ item in set A.
B_i is the presence (1) or absence (0) of the $i-th$ item in set B.
n is the total number of items (dimensions) in the sets.

Definition 2: (Similarity measure)

A similarity measure is generally expressed as a numerical value that increases as the resemblance between item sets A and B becomes greater. This measure is computed using the formula provided in Equation 5.2.

$$sim(A,B) = \frac{2 \times len(inter(A,B))}{len(A) + len(B)} \tag{5.2}$$

Where $len(inter)$ signifies the size of the intersection of the two item sets, and $len(A), len(B)$ represents the size of each individual item set. It's crucial to keep in mind that the size of an itemset reflects the count of items contained within that itemset. Considering that we are working with item sets and our goal is to evaluate the similarity between them, we focus on measuring the similarity between these sets. However, since we are introducing a clustering algorithm, a more suitable approach is to utilize a distance measure. Consequently, we have integrated both similarity measures into a unified metric called the FI-distance. This FI-distance is computed using Equation 5.3.

$$FI - distance(A,B) = \frac{len(A) + len(B)}{1 + 2 \times len(inter(A,B))} \times \sqrt{\sum_{i=1}^{i=n} (Ai - Bi)^2} \tag{5.3}$$

The FI-distance equation consists of two components. The first part on the left represents the similarity between two sets of items (Equation 5.2). However, since our goal is to minimize the similarity between item sets (centroids), we have utilized the reciprocal of Equation 5.2 To prevent division by zero, we have added a term of 1 in the denominators.

The second segment involves the calculation of the Euclidean distance (Equation 5.1). This merging of both similarity and Euclidean distance components integrates information from both measurements, thus facilitating

the grouping of data points into clusters. This fusion approach has the potential to enhance the overall quality of clustering results by taking into account various aspects of the data's relationships and characteristics.
After determining the centroids, CFI proceeds to initiate the clustering process by utilizing these computed centroids. To illustrate this with an example, CFI calculates the membership degree of a given record concerning each centroid and then assigns it to the cluster for which it holds the highest membership degree.

In situations where an object's maximum membership is evenly distributed between two centroids, it is assigned to the cluster whose centroid has the highest support value. Additionally, if the two centroids also possess equal support values, the object will be assigned to the centroid with the maximum size, i.e., the one that contains a greater number of items.

5.2.4 Degree of membership

This metric is expressed as a value within the range of 0 to 1. A value of 1 signifies that an object is a member of the centroid (item set), whereas values approaching 0 suggest that the object's association with a specific centroid is weak. The calculation of this metric is carried out using the following formula (Eq 5.4):

$$Degree_{Membership}(x_i, A) = \frac{1}{len(A)} \times \sum_{j=0}^{j=len(A)} x_{i,j} = A_j \tag{5.4}$$

Where x_i represents an object and A represents a centroid with the form of an item set.

5.2.5 The CFI-Algorithm

The algorithm we present outlines the precise steps of our developed approach, comprising three main functions:

1. **Frequent Itemset Generation Function**: This initial function focuses on generating frequent itemsets. It begins by converting all continuous attributes into categorical ones. Subsequently, it employs the FP-growth algorithm (Han et al., 2000) to identify these frequent itemsets. Afterward, it removes any subsets found within these identified frequent itemsets.
2. **Centroid Determination Function**: In contrast, the second function is designed to determine centroids from the frequent itemsets generated by the first function. The objective here is to optimize the FI-distance between centroids, ultimately maximizing the separation between them.
3. **Data Point Assignment Function**: The final function is responsible for assigning each data point to the appropriate cluster based on the degree of membership as outlined in Equation 5.4.

These three functions collectively define the key operations within our proposed algorithm.

Algorithm 5.1: The CFI-Algorithm

Input: A data set $D := (x_1, \ldots, x_n)$, minimum support min_{sup}, the number of clusters k
Output: cluster centroids

```
begin
    Function CreatefreqItemSets(D, min_sup):
        freqItemSets = ∅
        transform all continuous features into Intervals
        transform data set to transactional dataset
        freqItemSets = FP − growth(D, min_sup)
        eliminate subsets from freqItemSets
        order freqItemSets by support
        return freqItemSets

    Function CreateCentroids(freqItemSets, k):
        centroids = ∅
        itemset_1 = get the itemset with the max support
        centroids = centroids ∪ {itemset_1}
        while len(centroids) < k do
            for i = 1 to len(freqItemSets) do
                itemset_i = get the itemset with the max Fi-distance from
                  itemsets in centroids
            end
            centroids = centroids ∪ {itemset_i}
        end
        return centroids

    Function CreateClusters(D, centroids):
        clusters = ∅
        for each datapoint d from D do
            clusters = assign datapoint to closest centroid using Eq 5.4.
        end
        return clusters
end
```

5.2.6 Computational complexity

To assess the computational complexity of our algorithm, we will first ascertain the complexity of each individual step and subsequently combine them:

- **Initialization**: The complexity here is $O(n^2)$, where n represents the number of frequent itemsets.
- **Centroids Detection**: For each iteration, the complexity can be approximated as $O(n^2)$, with n being the number of frequent itemsets.

- **Stopping Condition**: The number of iterations hinges on factors such as the count of frequent itemsets and the chosen stopping condition.

The primary contributor to the overall complexity appears to be the centroids detection step, contributing $O(n^2)$ for each iteration. The total number of iterations is determined by the stopping condition. Assuming the number of iterations is p (influenced by various factors including the stopping condition), the cumulative complexity for centroids detection can be approximated as $O(p \times n^2)$.

The other steps initialization and stopping condition bear complexities of $O(n^2)$. Consequently, their contributions might also impact the overall complexity.

Considering the complexity approximation for frequent itemsets generation using the FP-growth (Han et al., 2000) ($O(k \times m^k)$), where k is the average size of frequent itemsets and m is the number of distinct items, the approximate overall computational complexity of your algorithm can be expressed as:

$$O(n^2 + p \times n^2 + k \times m^k) \tag{5.5}$$

5.3 Experimental Analysis

In this section, we conduct a comparative analysis between our developed approach and various clustering techniques. This comparison is structured into four main sections. The initial part offers insights into the clustering techniques employed in this study. The second section provides details about the datasets utilized in our research. Following that, the third part delves into the parameter configurations used. Lastly, the fourth section presents the experimental results and offers a relative analysis of the findings.

5.3.1 Methodology

To assess the efficacy of our approach, this section involves subjecting the proposed algorithm to testing using both real-world and synthetic datasets. We have conducted comparisons between our method and a selection of widely recognized clustering algorithms, which include the following popular choices:

- The spectral clustering method (SCM) (Luxburg, 2017)
- Clustering based on morphological operations (CMO) (Wang, 2020)
- The Ward agglomerative clustering method (WAC) (Xu and Tian, 2015)
- Clustering-based information retrieval using frequent closed itemsets (CIR) (Djenouri et al., 2018)

5.3.2 Datasets

This study compares the proposed clustering algorithms with four state-of-the-art methods using 16 datasets from two categories.

Artificial datasets: We consider four synthetic datasets. Table 5.1 contains the names of the datasets, the total number of data examples in each dataset, the total number of attributes in each data object, and the total number of clusters. A dataset named "Blobs" was created using an isotropic Gaussian function and contains five classes, 500 samples, and two features for each class. The three remaining simulated datasets are taken from (Fränti and Sieranoja, 2018).

Datasets in the UCI (Asuncion and Newman, 2007) and Kaggle repositories (Kaggle, 2024): twelve known real-world datasets were adopted, including Leaf, House, Iris, Yeast, Wine, Avila, E-shop, Seeds, Poker hand, Obesity, Ecoli, and Shuttle. Table 5.1 provides a summary of each of these datasets.

TABLE 5.1 – Datasets descriptions

Id	Category	Datasets			
		Dataset name	Size	Features size	Clusters size
1	Synthetic datasets	Flame	240	2	2
2		path	240	2	3
3		Jain	373	2	2
4		Blobs	500	2	5
5	UCI and Kaggle datasets	Leaf	340	15	30
6		Avila	10430	10	12
7		House	5493	3	6
8		Poker hand	25010	10	10
9		Iris	150	4	3
10		Ecoli	336	8	8
11		Seeds	210	7	3
12		Shuttle	43500	9	7
13		Wine	178	13	3
14		Obesity	2111	16	7
15		Yeast	1484	8	10
16		E-shop clothing	165473	13	5

5.3.3 Parameter settings

The main parameters for each of the mentioned clustering methods, along with their range of values are listed below:

1. **Spectral Clustering Method (SCM)** (Luxburg, 2017):
   - Similarity Metric: The measure of similarity between data points. Common options include Euclidean distance, cosine similarity, Gaussian kernel, etc.
2. **Clustering based on Morphological Operations (CMO)** (Wang, 2020):
   - Max Iterations: The maximum number of iterations for the morphological dilation process.
   - Distance Metric: The metric for calculating distances between data points, e.g., Euclidean distance.

3. **Ward Agglomerative Clustering Method (WAC)** (Xu and Tian, 2015):
   - Linkage Criterion: The criterion used to measure the distance between clusters during the merging process. Options include "ward" (minimizing variance increase), "single," "complete," "average," etc.
   - Distance Metric: The metric for calculating distances between data points within clusters, e.g., Euclidean distance.
4. **Cluster-based Information Retrieval using Frequent Closed Itemsets (CIR)** (Djenouri et al., 2018):
   - Minimum Support Threshold: The minimum proportion of documents a frequent closed itemset should appear in.
   - Maximum Itemset Size: The maximum number of terms allowed in a frequent closed itemset.
   - Similarity Measure: The measure used to assess the similarity between clusters or items, e.g., Jaccard similarity, cosine similarity.
5. **Clustering based on frequent itemsets (CFI)**
   - Minimum Support Threshold: It determines the minimum frequency (or count) an itemset must have in the dataset to be considered "frequent."
   - Intervals Size: This parameter determines how many intervals the data should be grouped into in the case of numerical features.

5.3.4 Results and discussions

In this study, we conducted two primary experiments. The first experiment involved applying all the algorithms outlined in Section 5.3.1 to the four datasets listed in Table 5.1. The results of this experiment are visualized in the following figures.

In the initial group of datasets, we utilized synthetic data where the clusters were pre-defined. The first dataset, known as the "flame dataset," is depicted in Figure 5.2, showcasing its clustering outcomes using various methods. The second dataset, referred to as the "Jain dataset," is displayed in Figure 5.3, revealing the clustering results obtained through diverse techniques. Subsequently, the third dataset, termed the "Path dataset," is showcased in Figure 5.4, illustrating its clustering outcomes under different methods. Finally, the last synthetic dataset within this experiment is labeled the "Blobs dataset," and Figure 5.5 displays its clustering results across distinct methods.

In our second experiment, we conducted a comparison between the CFI algorithm and four state-of-the-art methods using the real datasets displayed in Table 5.1. This comparison was based on the assessment of three performance metrics: the Davies Bouldin score (Table 5.2), the Silhouette Width Criterion (Table 5.3), and the Calinski-Harabasz score (Table 5.4). The results of this experiment are presented in the following tables.

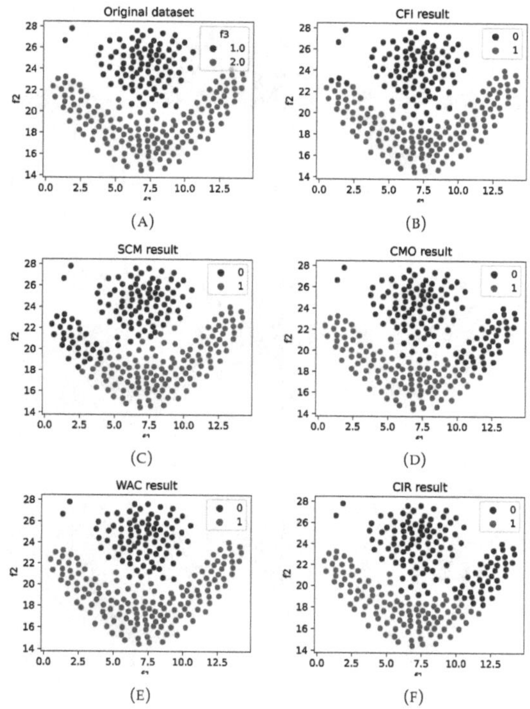

FIGURE 5.2 – Comparison of different clustering algorithms with the CFI method on the first synthetic dataset (flame). (a) the original dataset, (b) Result of CFI, (c) Result of SCM, (d) Result of CMO, (e) Result of WAC, (f) Result of SIR.

To validate the effectiveness of the CFI algorithm, we conducted supplementary experiments focusing on execution time, a crucial factor in performance enhancement. These experiments involved a comparative analysis of the execution time between the CFI algorithm and four state-of-the-art methods. We used the real datasets specified in Table 5.1 for these experiments. The results of these time-related comparisons are visually presented in Figure 5.6.

5.3.5 Results analysis

In Figure 5.2, it becomes evident that only the CFI method and WAC managed to accurately cluster the flame dataset. Shifting our focus to the second dataset (Figure 5.3), the WAC algorithm demonstrates the most proficient clustering performance. As we evaluate the performance of the other algorithms on the same dataset, they yield comparable and satisfactory outcomes. Advancing to the path dataset, as depicted in Figure 5.4, the CFI

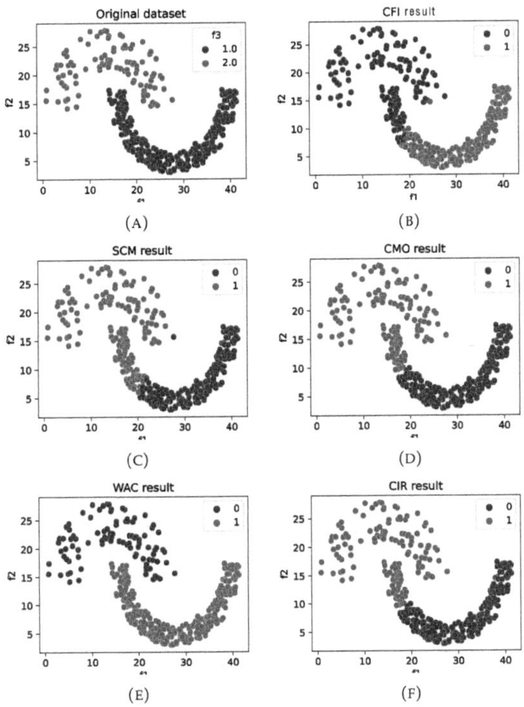

FIGURE 5.3 – Comparison of different clustering algorithms with the CFI method on the second synthetic dataset (Jain). (a) the original dataset, (b) Result of CFI, (c) Result of SCM, (d) Result of CMO, (e) Result of WAC, (f) Result of SIR.

algorithm exhibits the most superior clustering performance, while the remaining algorithms yield nearly indistinguishable results. Moving to the fourth dataset (Figure 5.5), a clear observation emerges wherein all algorithms proficiently cluster the dataset; however, the CFI algorithm's results display a slight deviation from those of the other algorithms.

Referring to Table 5.2, it becomes apparent that the CFI algorithm attains the highest performance in terms of the Davies-Bouldin index. This is evident as it surpasses its competitors on six out of the twelve datasets, culminating in the most favorable average score. Following closely, the SCM algorithm demonstrates exceptional performance, closely trailing the CFI algorithm across the majority of datasets. On the other hand, the remaining methods exhibit relatively more distant performance compared to the CFI and SCM algorithms.

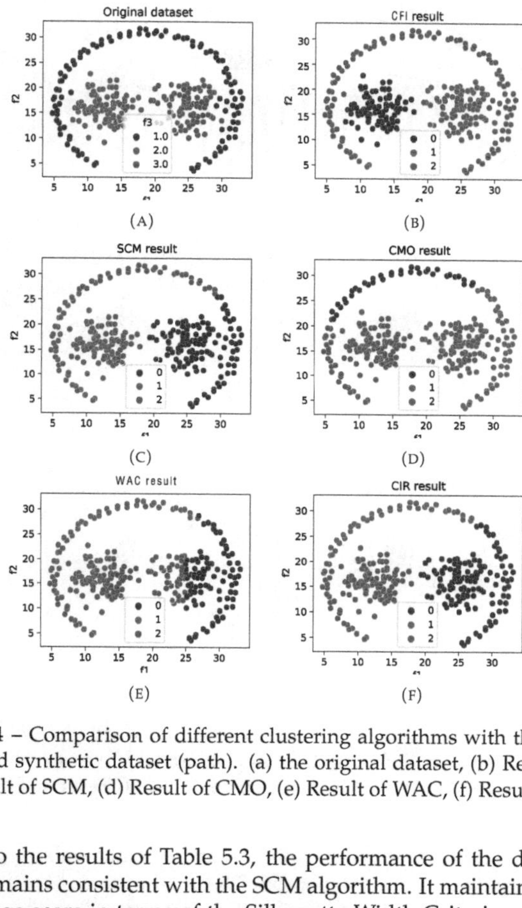

FIGURE 5.4 – Comparison of different clustering algorithms with the CFI method on the third synthetic dataset (path). (a) the original dataset, (b) Result of CFI, (c) Result of SCM, (d) Result of CMO, (e) Result of WAC, (f) Result of SIR.

Turning to the results of Table 5.3, the performance of the developed approach remains consistent with the SCM algorithm. It maintains the second-best average score in terms of the Silhouette Width Criterion while outperforming the competitors in four of the twelve datasets. Additionally, the score differences with the competitors for the remaining datasets are negligibly minor. CMO secures the third position, followed by WAC and CIR.

Regarding Table 5.4, it is evident that CFI outperforms the other algorithms on five of the twelve datasets in terms of the Calinski-Harabasz index. Consequently, the CFI algorithm achieves the highest average score. Furthermore, the variations in scores compared to competitors are virtually insignificant across the remaining datasets, with the exception of the 'e-shop' dataset. Within the same table, the SCM demonstrates strong performance, securing the second position. It is followed by WAC, CMO, and CIR, which occupy the subsequent positions.

From Figure 5.6, it's clear that the CFI algorithm is not the fastest clustering

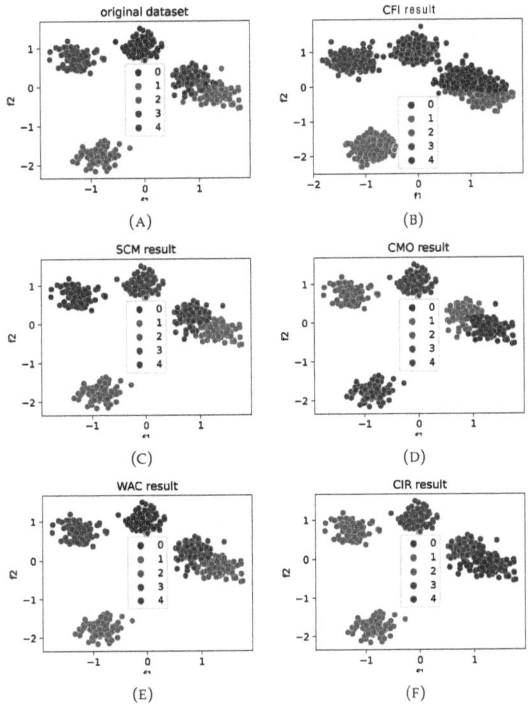

FIGURE 5.5 – Comparison of different clustering algorithms with the CFI method on the last synthetic dataset (blob). (a) the original dataset, (b) Result of CFI, (c) Result of SCM, (d) Result of CMO, (e) Result of WAC, (f) Result of SIR.

method. Still, it remains competitive in all datasets, with generally negligible differences compared to the fastest method. These differences become more noticeable only in the poker, shuttle, and e-shop datasets. This observation aligns with expectations since a significant portion of the execution time of the CFI method is dedicated to generating frequent item sets.

Overall, when considering all the previous experiments, the developed approach consistently demonstrates commendable performance when compared to state-of-the-art methods. This holds true regardless of whether synthetic or real datasets were employed and irrespective of the evaluation metric utilized.

5.4 Summary of the chapter

This work introduced a novel clustering algorithm rooted in the frequency-based approach, utilizing frequent item sets to construct clusters. The algorithm amalgamates a similarity measure and Euclidean distance to create

TABLE 5.2 – Comparison of the clustering algorithms with the CFI method according to the Davies-Bouldin index

id	CFI	SCM	CMO	WAC	CIR
5	**1.75**	1.81	1.78	1.90	1.83
6	3.21	**3.01**	3.47	3.04	3.22
7	**1.00**	1.16	1.31	1.25	1.61
8	**3.40**	3.55	4.69	3.51	4.59
9	**1.05**	1.10	1.06	2.48	1.43
10	2.21	2.45	2.65	**2.20**	2.41
11	**1.11**	1.17	1.19	1.17	1.38
12	2.28	2.17	**2.09**	2.19	2.48
13	2.08	**2.00**	1.99	2.03	2.08
14	2.57	**2.53**	2.78	2.59	2.84
15	2.83	2.53	2.65	**2.46**	3.16
16	**2.39**	2.50	2.56	2.61	2.48
Vectories	6	3	1	2	0
avg	**2.16**	2.17	2.35	2.28	2.46

a composite distance metric, which is then maximized to determine cluster centroids. A series of experiments, conducted across sixteen datasets, consistently demonstrated the superiority of the CFI algorithm. Evaluation was performed using three clustering metrics: the Davies Bouldin index, the Silhouette Width Criterion, and the Calinski-Harabasz score. Additionally, the algorithm's robustness was assessed through experiments with synthetic datasets.

Looking ahead, one promising avenue for future development involves integrating the CFI algorithm with established clustering techniques like k-means, hierarchical clustering, or density-based clustering. This hybrid approach has the potential to leverage the strengths of both methods, thereby enhancing overall performance.

Another research direction involves Dynamic Updating, focusing on methods to adapt frequent itemsets and clusters in response to the arrival of new data points. This concept holds significant promise for applications dealing with streaming data or scenarios where data distribution evolves over time.

Finally, an additional research path pertains to Incremental Clustering. Here, the aim is to modify the algorithm to accommodate incremental clustering, allowing for the seamless addition of new data points without requiring a complete reevaluation of existing clusters. This approach could substantially enhance efficiency and equip the algorithm to effectively handle larger datasets.

TABLE 5.3 – Comparison of the clustering algorithms with the CFI method according to the Silhouette Width Criterion

id	CFI	SCM	CMO	WAC	CIR
5	0.032	0.037	0.006.	**0.043**	0.004
6	0.124	0.152	**0.153**	0.140	0.153
7	**0.112**	0.059	0.031	0.045	0.027
8	**0.542**	0.520	0.472	0.463	0.470
9	**0.145**	0.123	0.111	0.093	0.102
10	**0.415**	0.392	0.383	0.396	0.339
11	0.122	**0.160**	0.127	0.156	0.106
12	0.173	**0.182**	0.177	0.178	0.174
13	0.075	**0.089**	0.064	0.055	0.062
14	0.084	**0.110**	0.096	0.109	0.075
15	0.092	**0.101**	0.077	0.068	0.083
16	0.350	**0.439**	0.415	0.285	0.316
Vectories	4	6	1	1	0
avg	0.189	**0.197**	0.176	0.169	0.159

TABLE 5.4 – Comparison of the clustering algorithms with the CFI method according to the Calinski-Harabasz index

id	CFI	SCM	CMO	WAC	CIR
5	495.9	548.3	338.7	**606.6**	324.6
6	22.6.7	22.4	**23.0**	21.6	21.7
7	**1015.6**	357.3	291.7	357.3	286.1
8	**2525.7**	2247.4	1806.6	1697.8	1714.6
9	19.9	**32.0**	30.0	25.5	28.4
10	**121.3**	110.0	105.3	112.4	86.4
11	**5696.4**	4562.5	4027.6	4242.3	2685.3
12	94.6	**101.0**	99.2	98.4	96.2
13	64.7	**75.3**	66.8	62.3	61.1
14	1284.5	**2881.2**	2650.4	2801.0	2228.7
15	21.2	**29.0**	25.4	23.2	26.0
16	**103.5**	87.8	79.5	48.2	49.6
vectories	5	5	1	1	0
avg	**955.5**	921.2	795.4	841.4	634.1

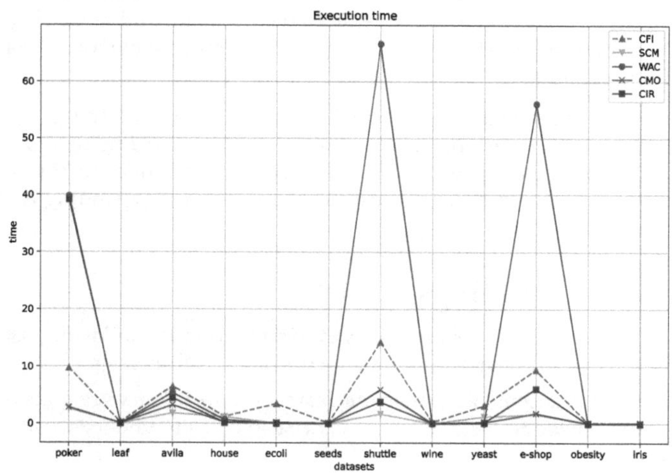

FIGURE 5.6 – The execution time (in seconds) of the different compared clustering methods.

Conclusion and Future Work

The field of machine learning poses significant challenges due to the constant influx of data from diverse sources and the wide array of existing algorithms and techniques. The primary objective of this thesis was to create innovative machine-learning algorithms that enhance the existing ones. These enhancements aimed to improve interpretability, simplify complexity, reduce storage requirements, and boost the performance of the designed models. The study also involved a thorough analysis and empirical comparisons to reveal the strengths and weaknesses of various machine learning methods. Furthermore, the intention was to offer readers and researchers a clear overview and guidelines for the appropriate implementation of machine learning techniques.

In this section, we outline the key conclusions drawn from our findings and provide insights into future prospects. The "Summary and findings" section encapsulates the essence of our work and its findings, while the "Future Work" section delves into potential research directions for expanding and building upon our findings.

Summary and findings

The main findings of the book are briefly summarized in the following list. A more detailed outline can be found in the upcoming subsections.

1. The latest advancements in machine learning algorithms were meticulously organized to offer readers a concise and easily understandable overview.
2. An empirical analysis was conducted, employing various machine learning algorithms across different categories, to thoroughly assess their applicability on both synthetic and real-world datasets.
3. Our primary focus was on researching and innovating new machine learning algorithms to tackle specific challenges discussed earlier.
4. We established a foundation for conducting unbiased comparisons among different machine learning algorithms.

Analyzing and evaluating machine learning state-of-the-art methods

In this book, we conducted a thorough and critical evaluation of various machine learning algorithms belonging to different categories, including ***Decision tree***, ***Random Forest***, and ***KNN*** as supervised learning methods, and ***Kmeans*** and ***Association rules*** as unsupervised learning techniques. Each of these methods was assessed in conjunction with well-established classifiers to systematically evaluate their ability to select the optimal classifier. Our empirical comparisons were performed across a diverse range of benchmarking datasets, highlighting the practical applicability of these machine learning algorithms.

The results obtained clearly demonstrate that there is no universally superior algorithm applicable to all datasets. Each algorithm exhibits varying performance levels depending on the specific problem, data type, size, and other criteria. Consequently, the selection of the most appropriate algorithm becomes crucial to achieve effective classification, gain valuable insights into the data, and improving generalization.

In addition to the empirical comparisons, we provided readers with an extensive overview of the entire machine learning framework. This comprehensive approach was designed to offer readers a clear understanding of the field of machine learning.

Developing new machine learning algorithms

Returning to the main goal of this book, we have proposed seven machine learning algorithms. First, we introduced a new decision tree pre-pruning method based on nodes probabilities, which stops creating decision tree nodes when their probabilities exceed a certain threshold.

Second, we presented a modified version of Decision Tree (DT) that enhances weak nodes using Data Augmentation. We introduced a new algorithm called Enhanced Weak Nodes in Decision Tree (EWNDT), which reinforces nodes containing few instances by augmenting their data from similar tree nodes. We utilized two approaches to measure the similarity between nodes. The results confirm that this technique improves the classification performance.

Third, we proposed a modified version of K-nearest neighbors (KNN) that uses association rules to estimate feature weighting. This enhanced KNN integrates association rules and information gains to assign weights to individual features in a dataset based on their relevance to the target attribute. By combining these techniques, the new weighting approach aims to enhance the performance of the KNN algorithm in various data analysis tasks.

Fourth, we introduced an ensemble method that utilizes KNN and feature correlation. The enhanced K-nearest neighbors (KNN) algorithm serves as a base learner within this ensemble method, combined with correlation-based feature subset selection. Experimental results demonstrate the superiority of our proposed algorithm over alternative machine learning methods.

Fifth, we proposed a modified version of the random forest classifier that uses association rule metrics to evaluate branches. This version incorporates a novel forest pruning strategy called PRM, relying on association rules metrics. The PRM approach involves extracting branches from the initial forest, evaluating each branch's score, and removing underperforming ones. The selected branches are then utilized to predict new data by aggregating their outcomes. Notably, this strategy can be extended to various types of tree ensembles.

Sixth, we introduced another modified version of random forest combined with Naïve Bayes to predict student performance. This innovative machine-learning algorithm merges Random Forest with Naïve Bayes to forecast student performance. The algorithm extracts branches from the forest and evaluates them using the posterior probability of Naïve Bayes to select an optimal subset of branches. This final subset of branches is used to predict student performance, and experimental results demonstrate the commendable performance of this approach.

Finally, we proposed a new clustering method that utilizes Frequent Item Sets. This innovative clustering approach centers around frequency and employs the Apriori algorithm to generate frequent elements. It selects k centers to maximize the difference between these centers using a new measure called the FI-distance, which combines the Euclidean distance and the similarity between item sets. This method offers a more robust clustering criterion and holds promise for improving the effectiveness and efficiency of clustering tasks across various domains.

Introducing an evaluation methodology of machine learning

We have established a solid foundation for a fair comparison of machine learning algorithms through several key measures. Firstly, we meticulously curated and presented more than thirteen classification benchmarking datasets. These datasets were deliberately chosen to be diverse, varying not only in the number of instances but also in the attributes, ensuring a comprehensive evaluation of the algorithms discussed earlier. To enhance the depth of our analysis, we complemented these real-world datasets with synthetic ones, leveraging their unique insights into algorithmic behavior.

Additionally, rigorous pre-processing steps were taken prior to the learning phase. This included addressing issues like missing data, outlier detection, and normalization techniques. By ensuring the quality and consistency of the data, we aimed to eliminate biases and confounding factors, thereby fostering a more accurate assessment of the algorithms' performances.

Furthermore, our approach encompassed the utilization of robust validation techniques and evaluation metrics. These metrics, such as Accuracy, AUC, Error estimate, Precision, and Recall, were employed to estimate the generalization performance of supervised learning models on unseen data. For clustering problems, metrics like Silhouette and Davies-Boudine score were utilized. By employing a wide array of evaluation criteria, we sought to capture the nuances of algorithmic effectiveness, providing a comprehensive and insightful analysis of their capabilities.

Future work

In our book work, we have identified several avenues for future research, opening up new perspectives at various levels within the field of machine learning. Here, we outline some of the most pressing questions and potential directions for further exploration:

1. **Random Forest Tree Pruning Techniques**: The pruning of random forest trees can be approached through a multitude of techniques. While our book explored two methods, there exists a rich landscape of dynamic approaches that could be investigated. Exploring and comparing different pruning strategies, including dynamic techniques, could significantly enhance the efficiency and accuracy of random forest models.
2. **Enhancing Decision Tree Algorithms**: Further improvements in the decision tree algorithm can be achieved by carefully selecting stopping criteria during the construction phase. While our book employed probability pre-pruning, future research could delve into using more sophisticated criteria, such as conditional probability. Investigating these criteria could lead to decision trees that are not only more accurate but also more adaptable to complex datasets.
3. **Extension of Association Rules for Feature Weighting**: We utilized association rules to estimate feature weights for the KNN algorithm. Extending this feature weighting technique to other machine learning algorithms, such as Support Vector Machines (SVM), holds great promise. Exploring the application of association rules in diverse contexts could uncover novel insights into optimizing feature selection for various algorithms, enhancing their predictive capabilities.
4. **Hybrid Clustering Approaches**: Integrating the CFI algorithm with established clustering techniques like k-means, hierarchical clustering, or density-based clustering represents an intriguing research avenue. This hybrid approach has the potential to harness the unique strengths of different methods, leading to more robust and accurate clustering results. Additionally, exploring the concept of Dynamic Updating in clustering algorithms could revolutionize their applicability, particularly in scenarios involving streaming data or evolving data distributions. Investigating methods to dynamically update frequent itemsets and clusters in response to new data points could significantly enhance the adaptability and real-time performance of clustering algorithms.

By addressing these open questions and exploring these research directions, future studies can contribute substantially to the advancement of machine learning techniques, leading to more sophisticated and effective models for various applications.

Publications of the Author

The research works carried out for the completion of this thesis work have resulted in several publications in national conferences, international conferences, and specialized journals. We present these publications next, sorting them by publication type.

International journals (#6)

- **Y. Manzali**, M. El Far, M. Chahhou and M. Elmohajir, (2022). Enhancing Weak Nodes in Decision Tree Algorithm Using Data Augmentation. Cybernetics and Information Technologies, 22(2), 50-65, https://doi.org/10.2478/cait-2022-0016
- **Y. Manzali** and M. El Far (2023). Random Forest Pruning Techniques: A Recent Review, Operations Research Forum, (Vol. 4, No. 2, pp. 1-14), Springer International Publishing. https://doi.org/10.1007/s43069-023-00223-6
- **Y. Manzali** and M. El Far (2024). Optimizing the number of branches in a decision forest using association rule metrics. Knowledge and Information Systems, 1-21. https://doi.org/10.1007/s10115-024-02069-8.
- **Y. Manzali**, K. A. Barry, Y. Balouki, R. Flouchi and M. El Far (2024).A feature weighted K-nearest neighbor algorithm based on association rules. Journal of Ambient Intelligence and Humanized Computing, 1-14. https://doi.org/10.1007/s12652-024-04793-z.
- **Y. Manzali**, K. A. Barry, Y. Balouki, R. Flouchi and M. El Far (2024).An innovative clustering approach utilizing frequent item sets. Multimedia Tools and Applications, 1-27. https://doi.org/10.1007/s11042-024-18913-6.
- **Y. Manzali**, Y. Akhiat, K. A. Barry, E. Akachar and M. El Far (2024). Prediction of Student Performance Using Random Forest Combined With Naïve Bayes. The Computer Journal, bxae036. https://doi.org/10.1093/comjnl/bxae036.

National conferences (#2)

- **Y. Manzali** and M. El Far, (2022). A new decision tree pre-pruning method based on nodes probabilities. In 2022 International Conference on Intelligent Systems and Computer Vision (ISCV) (pp. 1-5). IEEE. https://doi.org/10.1109/ISCV54655.2022.9806124
- **Y. Manzali**, K. A. Barry and M. El Far, "An Improved KNN Algorithm Based on Ensemble Methods and Correlation", 7TH IEEE Congress on

Information Science & Technology 2023 (CIST 2023)https://doi.org/10.1109/CiSt56084.2023.10409922

Bibliography

;.

Adnan, M.N., Islam, M.Z.. Optimizing the number of trees in a decision forest to discover a subforest with high ensemble accuracy using a genetic algorithm. Knowledge-Based Systems 2016;110:86–97.

Agrawal, R., Imielinski, T., Swami, A.. Mining association rules between sets of items in large databases. In: Proceedings of the 1993 ACM SIGMOD international conference on Management of data. 1993. p. 207–216.

Agrawal, R., Srikant, R., et al. Fast algorithms for mining association rules. In: Proc. 20th int. conf. very large data bases, VLDB. Santiago, Chile; volume 1215; 1994. p. 487–499.

Ahmed, A.M., Rizaner, A., Ulusoy, A.H.. A novel decision tree classification based on post-pruning with bayes minimum risk. Plos one 2018;13(4):e0194168.

Ajibade, S.S.M., Bahiah Binti Ahmad, N., Mariyam Shamsuddin, S.. Educational data mining: enhancement of student performance model using ensemble methods. In: IOP Conference Series: Materials Science and Engineering. IOP Publishing; volume 551; 2019. p. 012061.

Ajibade, S.S.M., Dayupay, J., Ngo-Hoang, D.L., Oyebode, O.J., Sasan, J.M., et al. Utilization of ensemble techniques for prediction of the academic performance of students. Journal of Optoelectronics Laser 2022;41(6):48–54.

Alamri, R., Alharbi, B.. Explainable student performance prediction models: a systematic review. IEEE Access 2021;9:33132–33143.

AlSukker, A., Khushaba, R., Al-Ani, A.. Optimizing the k-nn metric weights using differential evolution. In: 2010 International Conference on Multimedia Computing and Information Technology (MCIT). IEEE; 2010. p. 89–92.

Altman, N.S.. An introduction to kernel and nearest-neighbor nonparametric regression. The American Statistician 1992;46(3):175–185.

Amit, Y., Blanchard, G.. Multiple randomized classifiers: Mrcl 2001;.

Amit, Y., Geman, D.. Shape quantization and recognition with randomized trees. Neural computation 1997;9(7):1545–1588.

Anyanwu, M.N., Shiva, S.G., et al. Comparative analysis of serial decision tree classification algorithms. International Journal of Computer Science and Security 2009;3(3):230–240.

Asuncion, A., Newman, D.. Uci machine learning repository. 2007.

Bader-El-Den, M., Gaber, M.. Garf: towards self-optimised random forests. In: International conference on neural information processing. Springer; 2012. p. 506–515.

Banfield, R.E., Hall, L.O., Bowyer, K.W., Kegelmeyer, W.P.. A new ensemble diversity measure applied to thinning ensembles. In: International Workshop on Multiple Classifier Systems. Springer; 2003. p. 306–316.

Banfield, R.E., Hall, L.O., Bowyer, K.W., Kegelmeyer, W.P.. A comparison of decision tree ensemble creation techniques. IEEE transactions on pattern analysis and machine intelligence 2006;29(1):173–180.

Baradwaj, B.K., Pal, S.. Mining educational data to analyze students' performance. arXiv preprint arXiv:12013417 2012;.

Barlow, H.B.. Unsupervised learning. Neural computation 1989;1(3):295–311. URL: http://mlg.eng.cam.ac.uk/zoubin/course03/lect7mcmc.pdf.

Bauer, E., Kohavi, R.. An empirical comparison of voting classification algorithms: Bagging, boosting, and variants. Machine learning 1999;36(1):105–139.

Benediktsson, J.A., Kittler, J., Roli, F.. Multiple Classifier Systems: 8th International Workshop, MCS 2009, Reykjavik, Iceland, June 10-12, 2009, Proceedings. volume 5519. Springer, 2009.

Bhattacharya, G., Ghosh, K., Chowdhury, A.S.. Granger causality driven ahp for feature weighted knn. Pattern Recognition 2017;66:425–436.

Biswas, N., Chakraborty, S., Mullick, S.S., Das, S.. A parameter independent fuzzy weighted k-nearest neighbor classifier. Pattern Recognition Letters 2018;101:80–87.

Breiman, L.. Bagging predictors. Machine learning 1996;24(2):123–140.

Breiman, L.. Random forests. Machine learning 2001;45(1):5–32.

Breiman, L.. Consistency of random forests and other averaging classifiers. Technical Report; Technical Report; 2004.

Breiman, L., Friedman, J., Stone, C.J., Olshen, R.A.. Classification and regression trees. CRC press, 1984.

Breitenbach, M., Nielsen, R., Grudic, G.Z.. Probabilistic random forests: Predicting data point specific misclassification probabilities. Univ of Colorado at Boulder, Tech Rep CU-CS-954-03 2003;.

Breslow, L.A., Aha, D.W.. Simplifying decision trees: A survey. Knowledge engineering review 1997;12(1):1–40. URL: https://www.semanticscholar.org/paper/Simplifying-decision-trees%3A-A-survey-Breslow-Aha/a0e3e28c7635e69a1418d09030fcbdc2ff49a517?p2df.

Brown, G., Wyatt, J., Harris, R., Yao, X.. Diversity creation methods: a survey and categorisation. Information fusion 2005;6(1):5–20.

Bryll, R., Gutierrez-Osuna, R., Quek, F.. Attribute bagging: improving accuracy of classifier ensembles by using random feature subsets. Pattern recognition 2003;36(6):1291–1302.

Chen, Y., Hao, Y.. A feature weighted support vector machine and k-nearest neighbor algorithm for stock market indices prediction. Expert Systems with Applications 2017;80:340–355.

Chung, D., Kim, H.. Accurate ensemble pruning with pl-bagging. Computational Statistics & Data Analysis 2015;83:1–13.

Cortes, C., Vapnik, V.. Support-vector networks. Machine learning 1995;20:273–297.

Cover, T., Hart, P.. k-nearest neighbors algorithm. Pattern Analysis and Machine Intelligence 1967a;8(6):1–8.

Cover, T.M., Hart, P.E.. Nearest neighbor pattern classification. IEEE Transactions on Information Theory 1967b;13.

Daho, M.E.H., Settouti, N., Bechar, M.E.A., Boublenza, A., Chikh, M.A.. A new correlation-based approach for ensemble selection in random forests. International Journal of Intelligent Computing and Cybernetics 2021;.

Dasarathy, B.V.. A special issue on diversity in multiple classifier systems. Information Fusion 2005;6(1):1–1.

Davis, J.V., Kulis, B., Jain, P., Sra, S., Dhillon, I.S.. Information-theoretic metric learning. In: Proceedings of the 24th international conference on Machine learning. 2007. p. 209–216.

Defays, D.. An efficient algorithm for a complete link method. The Computer Journal 1977;20(4):364–366.

Dempster, A.P., Laird, N.M., Rubin, D.B.. Maximum likelihood from incomplete data via the em algorithm. Journal of the Royal Statistical Society: Series B (Methodological) 1977;39(1):1–22.

Derrac, J., García, S., Herrera, F.. Fuzzy nearest neighbor algorithms: Taxonomy, experimental analysis and prospects. Information Sciences 2014;260:98–119.

Dheenadayalan, K., Srinivasaraghavan, G., Muralidhara, V.. Pruning a random forest by learning a learning algorithm. In: International Conference on Machine Learning and Data Mining in Pattern Recognition. Springer; 2016. p. 516–529.

Dietterich, T.G.. Ensemble methods in machine learning. In: International workshop on multiple classifier systems. Springer; 2000a. p. 1–15.

Dietterich, T.G.. An experimental comparison of three methods for constructing ensembles of decision trees: Bagging, boosting, and randomization. Machine learning 2000b;40(2):139–157.

Dietterich, T.G., Bakiri, G.. Error-correcting output codes: a general method for improving multiclass inductive learning programs. In: Proceedings of the ninth National conference on Artificial intelligence-Volume 2. 1991. p. 572–577.

Djenouri, Y., Belhadi, A., Fournier-Viger, P., Lin, J.C.W.. Fast and effective cluster-based information retrieval using frequent closed itemsets. Information Sciences 2018;453:154–167.

Doan, M.T., Qi, J., Rajasegarar, S., Leckie, C.. Scalable bottom-up subspace clustering using fp-trees for high dimensional data. In: 2018 IEEE International Conference on Big Data (Big Data). IEEE; 2018. p. 106–111.

Domingos, P., Hulten, G.. Beyond bagging: Boosting and categorizing. Proceedings of the Seventeenth International Conference on Machine Learning (ICML) 2000;.

Duda, R., Hart, P.. andd. g. stork, pattern classification. hoboken. 2001.

Efron, B., Tibshirani, R.J.. An introduction to the bootstrap. CRC press, 1994.

Esposito, F., Malerba, D., Semeraro, G., Kay, J.. A comparative analysis of methods for pruning decision trees. IEEE transactions on pattern analysis and machine intelligence 1997;19(5):476–491. URL: https://ieeexplore.ieee.org/abstract/document/589207.

Fahad, L.G., Tahir, S.F.. Activity recognition in a smart home using local feature weighting and variants of nearest-neighbors classifiers. Journal of Ambient Intelligence and Humanized Computing 2021;12:2355–2364.

Fairhurst, M., Rahman, F., et al. Special issue on multiple classifiers for document analysis applications. 1990.

Fawagreh, K., Gaber, M.M.. egap: An evolutionary game theoretic approach to random forest pruning. Big Data and Cognitive Computing 2020;4(4):37.

Fore, N.K.. A contrast pattern based clustering algorithm for categorical data 2010;.

Fränti, P., Sieranoja, S.. K-means properties on six clustering benchmark datasets. Applied intelligence 2018;48:4743–4759.

Freund, Y., Schapire, R.E.. A decision-theoretic generalization of online learning and an application to boosting. Journal of Computer and System Sciences 1997;55(1):119–139.

Freund, Y., Schapire, R.E., et al. Experiments with a new boosting algorithm. In: icml. Citeseer; volume 96; 1996. p. 148–156.

Friedman, J.H.. Stochastic gradient boosting. Computational statistics & data analysis 2002;38(4):367–378.

Ganaie, M., Tanveer, M., Suganthan, P.N.. Oblique decision tree ensemble via twin bounded svm. Expert Systems with Applications 2020;143:113072.

Garcia-Laencina, P.J., Sancho-Gomez, J.L., Figueiras-Vidal, A.R., Verleysen, M.. K nearest neighbours with mutual information for simultaneous classification and missing data imputation. Neurocomputing 2009;72(7-9):1483–1493.

Giffon, L., Lamothe, C., Bouscarrat, L., Milanesi, P., Cherfaoui, F., Koco, S.. Pruning random forest with orthogonal matching trees 2020;.

Gong, C., Su, Z.g., Wang, P.h., Wang, Q., You, Y.. Evidential instance selection for k-nearest neighbor classification of big data. International Journal of Approximate Reasoning 2021;138:123–144.

Grabowski, S.. Voting over multiple k-nn classifiers. In: Modern problems of radio engineering, telecommunications and computer science (IEEE Cat. No. 02EX542). IEEE; 2002. p. 223–225.

Grandvalet, Y.. Bagging equalizes influence. Machine Learning 2004;55(3):251–270.

Gul, A., Perperoglou, A., Khan, Z., Mahmoud, O., Miftahuddin, M., Adler, W., Lausen, B.. Ensemble of a subset of k nn classifiers. Advances in data analysis and classification 2018;12:827–840.

Gutierrez-Rodríguez, A.E., Martínez-Trinidad, J.F., García-Borroto, M., Carrasco-Ochoa, J.A.. Mining patterns for clustering on numerical datasets using unsupervised decision trees. Knowledge-Based Systems 2015a;82:70–79.

Gutierrez-Rodríguez, A.E., Martínez-Trinidad, J.F., García-Borroto, M., Carrasco-Ochoa, J.A.. Mining patterns for clustering using unsupervised decision trees. Intelligent Data Analysis 2015b;19(6):1297–1310.

Haindl, M., Kittler, J., Roli, F.. Multiple Classifier Systems: 7th International Workshop, MCS 2007, Prague, Czech Republic, May 23-25, 2007, Proceedings. volume 4472. Springer, 2007.

Han, J., Kamber, M., Pei, J.. Data mining: Concepts and. Techniques, Waltham: Morgan Kaufmann Publishers 2012;.

Han, J., Pei, J., Yin, Y.. Mining frequent patterns without candidate generation. ACM sigmod record 2000;29(2):1–12.

Hart, P.E., Stork, D.G., Duda, R.O.. Pattern classification. Wiley Hoboken, 2000.

Ho, T., decision Forest, R.. Document analysis and recognition, 1995. In: Proceedings of the third international conference on. volume 1; 1995. p. 278–282.

Ho, T.K.. A Theory of Multiple Classi er Systems And Its Application to Visual Word Recognition. Ph.D. thesis; Citeseer; 1992.

Ho, T.K.. Random decision forests. In: Proceedings of 3rd international conference on document analysis and recognition. IEEE; volume 1; 1995. p. 278–282.

Ho, T.K.. The random subspace method for constructing decision forests. IEEE transactions on pattern analysis and machine intelligence 1998;20(8):832–844.

Hosmer Jr, D.W., Lemeshow, S., Sturdivant, R.X.. Applied logistic regression. volume 398. John Wiley & Sons, 2013.

Hssina, B., Merbouha, A., Ezzikouri, H., Erritali, M.. A comparative study of decision tree id3 and c4. 5. International Journal of Advanced Computer Science and Applications 2014;4(2):13–19.

Hsu, C.W., Lin, C.J.. A comparison of methods for multiclass support vector machines. IEEE transactions on Neural Networks 2002;13(2):415–425.

Hu, D., Liu, Q., Yan, Q.. Decision tree merging branches algorithm based on equal predictability. In: 2009 International Conference on Artificial Intelligence and Computational Intelligence. IEEE; volume 3; 2009. p. 214–218.

Hu, R., Zhou, S., Liu, Y., Tang, Z.. Margin-based pareto ensemble pruning: An ensemble pruning algorithm that learns to search optimized ensembles. Computational Intelligence and Neuroscience 2019;2019.

Huang, G.B., Zhou, H., Ding, X., Zhang, R.. Extreme learning machine for regression and multiclass classification. IEEE Transactions on Systems, Man, and Cybernetics, Part B (Cybernetics) 2011;42(2):513–529.

Huang, J., Wei, Y., Yi, J., Liu, M.. An improved knn based on class contribution and feature weighting. In: 2018 10th international conference on measuring technology and mechatronics automation (ICMTMA). IEEE; 2018. p. 313–316.

Huang, Z.. Clustering large data sets with mixed numeric and categorical values. In: Proceedings of the 1st pacific-asia conference on knowledge discovery and data mining,(PAKDD). Citeseer; 1997a. p. 21–34.

Huang, Z.. A fast clustering algorithm to cluster very large categorical data sets in data mining. Dmkd 1997b;3(8):34–39.

Hunt, E.B., Marin, J., Stone, P.J.. Experiments in induction. 1966;.

Ignatov, D., Ignatov, A.. Decision stream: Cultivating deep decision trees. In: 2017 ieee 29th international conference on tools with artificial intelligence (ictai). IEEE; 2017. p. 905–912.

Jiang, X., Wu, C.a., Guo, H.. Forest pruning based on branch importance. Computational intelligence and neuroscience 2017;2017.

Kaggle, . Kaggle datasets platform. 2024. URL: `https://www.kaggle.com/datasets`; accessed: 2025-01-16.

Kasemtaweechok, C., Suwannik, W.. Adaptive geometric median prototype selection method for k-nearest neighbors classification. Intelligent Data Analysis 2019;23(4):855–876.

Kass, G.V.. An exploratory technique for investigating large quantities of categorical data. Journal of the Royal Statistical Society: Series C (Applied Statistics) 1980;29(2):119–127.

Keller, J.M., Gray, M.R., Givens, J.A.. A fuzzy k-nearest neighbor algorithm. IEEE transactions on systems, man, and cybernetics 1985;(4):580–585.

Kettler, J., Roli, F.. Multiple classifier systems 2000;.

Khan, Z., Gul, A., Perperoglou, A., Miftahuddin, M., Mahmoud, O., Adler, W., Lausen, B.. Ensemble of optimal trees, random forest and random projection ensemble classification. Advances in Data Analysis and Classification 2020;14(1):97–116.

Kittler, J., Roli, F.. Proceedings of the second international workshop on multiple classifier systems. 2001.

Kohavi, R., John, G.H.. Wrappers for feature subset selection. Artificial intelligence 1997;97(1-2):273–324.

Kumutha, V., Palaniammal, S.. An enhanced approach on handling missing values using bagging k-nn imputation. In: 2013 International Conference on Computer Communication and Informatics. IEEE; 2013. p. 1–8.

Kuncheva, L.I.. That elusive diversity in classifier ensembles. In: Iberian conference on pattern recognition and image analysis. Springer; 2003. p. 1126–1138.

Kuncheva, L.I.. Combining pattern classifiers: methods and algorithms. John Wiley & Sons, 2014.

Kuncheva, L.I., Whitaker, C.J.. Measures of diversity in classifier ensembles and their relationship with the ensemble accuracy. Machine learning 2003;51(2):181–207.

Kuncheva, L.I., Whitaker, C.J., Shipp, C.A., Duin, R.P.. Is independence good for combining classifiers? In: Proceedings 15th International Conference on Pattern Recognition. ICPR-2000. IEEE; volume 2; 2000. p. 168–171.

Kuok, C.M., Fu, A., Wong, M.H.. Mining fuzzy association rules in databases. ACM Sigmod Record 1998;27(1):41–46.

Kurita, T.. An efficient agglomerative clustering algorithm using a heap. Pattern Recognition 1991;24(3):205–209.

Latinne, P., Debeir, O., Decaestecker, C.. Mixing bagging and multiple feature subsets to improve classification accuracy of decision tree combination. In: BENE-LEARN 2000, Tenth Belgian-Dutch Conference on Machine Learning. .; 2000. .

Latinne, P., Debeir, O., Decaestecker, C.. Combining different methods and numbers of weak decision trees. Pattern Analysis & Applications 2002;5(2):201–209.

Lei, Y., Zuo, M.J.. Gear crack level identification based on weighted k nearest neighbor classification algorithm. Mechanical Systems and Signal Processing 2009;23(5):1535–1547.

Loyola-Gonzalez, O., Gutierrez-Rodríguez, A.E., Medina-Pérez, M.A., Monroy, R., Martínez-Trinidad, J.F., Carrasco-Ochoa, J.A., Garcia-Borroto, M.. An explainable artificial intelligence model for clustering numerical databases. IEEE Access 2020;8:52370–52384.

Luna, J.M., Gennatas, E.D., Ungar, L.H., Eaton, E., Diffenderfer, E.S., Jensen, S.T., Simone, C.B., Friedman, J.H., Solberg, T.D., Valdes, G.. Building more accurate decision trees with the additive tree. Proceedings of the national academy of sciences 2019;116(40):19887–19893.

Luxburg, U.v.. A tutorial on spectral clustering. Statistics and Computing 2017;17(4):395–416.

MacQueen, J.. Classification and analysis of multivariate observations. In: 5th Berkeley Symp. Math. Statist. Probability. 1967. p. 281–297.

MacQueen, J., et al. Some methods for classification and analysis of multivariate observations. In: Proceedings of the fifth Berkeley symposium on mathematical statistics and probability. Oakland, CA, USA; volume 1; 1967. p. 281–297. URL: `https://www.cs.cmu.edu/~bhiksha/courses/mlsp.fall2010/class14/macqueen.pdf`.

Mahfouz, M.A., Shoukry, A., Ismail, M.A.. Eknn: Ensemble classifier incorporating connectivity and density into knn with application to cancer diagnosis. Artificial Intelligence in Medicine 2021;111:101985.

Mahmood, A.M., Mrithyumjaya, P.G.V.G.K., Kuppa, R.. A new pruning approach for better and compact decision trees. International Journal on Computer Science & Engineering 2010;2(8):2551–2558.

Malerba, D., Esposito, F., Semeraro, G.. A further comparison of simplification methods for decision-tree induction. In: Learning from data. Springer; 1996. p. 365–374. URL: `https://citeseerx.ist.psu.edu/viewdoc/download?doi=10.1.1.48.5671&rep=rep1&type=pdf`.

Malika, C., Ghazzali, N., Boiteau, V., Niknafs, A.. Nbclust: an r package for determining the relevant number of clusters in a data set. J Stat Softw 2014;61:1–36. URL: `https://www.jstatsoft.org/article/view/v061i06`.

Manzali, Y., Chahhou, M., Mohajir, M.E.. Classification algorithm using branches importance. Neural Processing Letters 2021;:1–17.

Martinez, W.G.. Ensemble pruning via quadratic margin maximization. IEEE Access 2021;9:48931–48951.

McLachlan, G.J., Basford, K.E.. Mixture models. inference and applications to clustering. Statistics: Textbooks and Monographs 1988;.

Mehanovic, D., Masetic, Z., Keco, D.. Prediction of heart diseases using majority voting ensemble method. In: CMBEBIH 2019: Proceedings of the International Conference on Medical and Biological Engineering, 16-18 May 2019, Banja Luka, Bosnia and Herzegovina. Springer; 2020. p. 491–498.

Mingers, J.. An empirical comparison of selection measures for decision-tree induction. Machine learning 1989;3(4):319–342.

Mining, W.I.D.. Data mining: Concepts and techniques. Morgan Kaufinann 2006;10:559–569.

Minsky, M.L.. Logical versus analogical or symbolic versus connectionist or neat versus scruffy. AI magazine 1991;12(2):34–34.

Mishra, N., Ron, D., Swaminathan, R.. A new conceptual clustering framework. Machine Learning 2004;56:115–151.

Montgomery, D.C.. Introduction to linear regression analysis. Technical Report; 1982.

Murthy, S.K.. Automatic construction of decision trees from data: A multi-disciplinary survey. Data mining and knowledge discovery 1998;2(4):345–389.

Namoun, A., Alshanqiti, A.. Predicting student performance using data mining and learning analytics techniques: A systematic literature review. Applied Sciences 2020;11(1):237.

Narassiguin, A., Elghazel, H., Aussem, A.. Similarity tree pruning: a novel dynamic ensemble selection approach. In: 2016 IEEE 16th International Conference on Data Mining Workshops (ICDMW). IEEE; 2016. p. 1243–1250.

de Nijs, J.. Decision dags–a new approach. cs brown edu 2011;.

Nilsson, N.J.. Learning machines. 1965;.

Olson, C.F.. Parallel algorithms for hierarchical clustering. Parallel computing 1995;21(8):1313–1325.

Onan, A.. A fuzzy-rough nearest neighbor classifier combined with consistency-based subset evaluation and instance selection for automated diagnosis of breast cancer. Expert Systems with Applications 2015;42(20):6844–6852.

Oza, N.C., Polikar, R., Kittler, J., Roli, F.. Multiple Classifier Systems: 6th International Workshop, MCS 2005, Seaside, CA, USA, June 13-15, 2005, Proceedings. volume 3541. Springer, 2005.

Pfahringer, B., Holmes, G., Kirkby, R.. New options for hoeffding trees. In: Australasian Joint Conference on Artificial Intelligence. Springer; 2007. p. 90–99.

Quinlan, J.R.. Induction of decision trees. Machine learning 1986;1(1):81–106. URL: https://link.springer.com/article/10.1007/BF00116251.

Quinlan, J.R.. Simplifying decision trees. International journal of man-machine studies 1987;27(3):221–234.

Quinlan, J.R.. C 4.5: Programs for machine learning. The Morgan Kaufmann Series in Machine Learning 1993;.

Ralambondrainy, H.. A conceptual version of the k-means algorithm. Pattern Recognition Letters 1995;16(11):1147–1157.

Rastrollo-Guerrero, J.L., Gómez-Pulido, J.A., Durán-Domínguez, A.. Analyzing and predicting students' performance by means of machine learning: A review. Applied sciences 2020;10(3):1042.

Ren, S., Cao, X., Wei, Y., Sun, J.. Global refinement of random forest. In: Proceedings of the IEEE Conference on Computer Vision and Pattern Recognition. 2015. p. 723–730.

Robnik-Šikonja, M.. Improving random forests. In: European conference on machine learning. Springer; 2004. p. 359–370.

Rodríguez-Fdez, I., Canosa, A., Mucientes, M., Bugarín, A.. Stac: a web platform for the comparison of algorithms using statistical tests. In: 2015 IEEE international conference on fuzzy systems (FUZZ-IEEE). IEEE; 2015. p. 1–8.

Roli, F., Kittler, J.. Fusion of multiple classifiers. Information Fusion 2002a;3(4):243–243.

Roli, F., Kittler, J.. Multiple Classifier Systems: Third International Workshop, MCS 2002, Cagliari, Italy, June 24-26, 2002. Proceedings. volume 2364. Springer Science & Business Media, 2002b.

Roli, F., Kittler, J.. Multiple Classifier Systems: 5th International Workshop, MCS 2004, Cagliari, Italy, June 9-11, 2004, Proceedings. volume 5. Springer Science & Business Media, 2004.

Schapire, R.E.. The strength of weak learnability. Machine learning 1990;5(2):197–227.

Scherf, M., Brauer, W.. Feature selection by means of a feature weighting approach. Citeseer, 1997.

Sebbanü, M., NockO, R., Chauchat, J., Rakotomalala, R.. Impact of learning set quality and size on decision tree performances. IJCSS 2000;1(1):85. URL: https://www.researchgate.net/profile/Jean-Hugues-Chauchat-3/publication/220316605_Impact_of_learning_set_quality_and_size_on_decision_tree_performances/links/02bfe510777f16ca25000000/Impact-of-learning-set-quality-and-size-on-decision-tree-performances.pdf.

Shamrat, F.J.M., Chakraborty, S., Billah, M.M., Das, P., Muna, J.N., Ranjan, R.. A comprehensive study on pre-pruning and post-pruning methods of decision tree classification algorithm. In: 2021 5th International conference on trends in electronics and informatics (ICOEI). IEEE; 2021. p. 1339–1345.

Shlien, S.. Multiple binary decision tree classifiers. Pattern Recognition 1990;23(7):757–763.

Sibson, R.. Slink: an optimally efficient algorithm for the single-link cluster method. The computer journal 1973;16(1):30–34.

Singh, S., Gupta, P.. Comparative study id3, cart and c4. 5 decision tree algorithm: a survey. International Journal of Advanced Information Science and Technology (IJAIST) 2014;27(27):97–103.

Sinta, D., Wijayanto, H., Sartono, B.. Ensemble k-nearest neighbors method to predict rice price in indonesia. Appl Math Sci 2014;8(160):7993–8005.

Skurichina, M.. Stabilizing weak classifiers. Regularization and Combining Techniques In Discriminant Analysis 2001;.

SOUAD, T.Z., ABDELKADER, A.. Pruning of random forests: a diversity-based heuristic measure to simplify a random forest ensemble. INFOCOMP: Journal of Computer Science 2019;18(1).

Su, M.Y.. Real-time anomaly detection systems for denial-of-service attacks by weighted k-nearest-neighbor classifiers. Expert Systems with Applications 2011;38(4):3492–3498.

Sutton, R.S., Barto, A.G., et al. Introduction to reinforcement learning. volume 135. MIT press Cambridge, 1998. URL: https://login.cs.utexas.edu/sites/default/files/legacy_files/research/documents/1%20intro%20up%20to%20RL%3ATD.pdf.

Swarna, K., Vinayagam, A., Ananth, M.B.J., Kumar, P.V., Veerasamy, V., Radhakrishnan, P.. A knn based random subspace ensemble classifier for detection and discrimination of high impedance fault in pv integrated power network. Measurement 2022;187:110333.

Tan, P.J., Dowe, D.L.. Mml inference of decision graphs with multi-way joins. In: Australian Joint Conference on Artificial Intelligence. Springer; 2002. p. 131–142.

Tang, B., He, H.. Enn: Extended nearest neighbor method for pattern recognition [research frontier]. IEEE Computational intelligence magazine 2015;10(3):52–60.

Tran, Q.N.. Classification, novelty detection and clustering for point pattern data. Ph.D. thesis; Curtin University; 2017.

Triguero, I., Derrac, J., Garcia, S., Herrera, F.. A taxonomy and experimental study on prototype generation for nearest neighbor classification. IEEE Transactions on Systems, Man, and Cybernetics, Part C (Applications and Reviews) 2011;42(1):86–100.

Tsang, I.W., Cheung, P.M., Kwok, J.T.. Kernel relevant component analysis for distance metric learning. In: Proceedings. 2005 IEEE International Joint Conference on Neural Networks, 2005. IEEE; volume 2; 2005. p. 954–959.

Tsymbal, A., Pechenizkiy, M., Cunningham, P.. Dynamic integration with random forests. In: European conference on machine learning. Springer; 2006. p. 801–808.

Uther, W.T., Veloso, M.M.. The lumberjack algorithm for learning linked decision forests. In: International Symposium on Abstraction, Reformulation, and Approximation. Springer; 2000. p. 219–232.

Wang, S., Jin, R.. An information geometry approach for distance metric learning. In: Artificial intelligence and statistics. PMLR; 2009. p. 591–598.

Wang, Z.. A new clustering method based on morphological operations. Expert Systems with Applications 2020;145:113102.

Weinberger, K.Q., Saul, L.K.. Distance metric learning for large margin nearest neighbor classification. Journal of machine learning research 2009;10(2).

Windeatt, T., Roli, F.. Multiple Classifier Systems: 4th International Workshop, MCS 2003, Guilford, UK, June 11-13, 2003, Proceedings. volume 2709. Springer, 2003.

Wolpert, D.H., Macready, W.G.. No free lunch theorems for optimization. IEEE transactions on evolutionary computation 1997;1(1):67–82.

Wong, A.K., Li, G.C.. Simultaneous pattern and data clustering for pattern cluster analysis. IEEE Transactions on Knowledge and Data Engineering 2008;20(7):911–923.

Wright, R.E.. Logistic regression. 1995;URL: `https://psycnet.apa.org/record/1995-97110-007`.

Wu, C.C., Chen, Y.L., Liu, Y.H., Yang, X.Y.. Decision tree induction with a constrained number of leaf nodes. Applied Intelligence 2016;45(3):673–685.

WU, X.w., SHI, B.n.. New algorithm of simplifying the id3 decision tree [j]. Journal of Hefei University of Technology (Natural Science) 2004;12.

Xiao, J.. Svm and knn ensemble learning for traffic incident detection. Physica A: Statistical Mechanics and its Applications 2019;517:29–35.

Xie, P., Xing, E.. Large scale distributed distance metric learning. arXiv preprint arXiv:14125949 2014;.

Xu, D., Tian, Y.. A comprehensive survey of clustering algorithms. Annals of Data Science 2015;2:165–193.

Yang, C., Wang, X., Zhu, R.. A strategy of merging branches based on margin enlargement of svm in decision tree induction. In: 2006 IEEE International Conference on Systems, Man and Cybernetics. IEEE; volume 1; 2006. p. 824–828.

Yang, H., Fong, S.. Incrementally optimized decision tree for noisy big data. In: Proceedings of the 1st International Workshop on Big Data, Streams and Heterogeneous Source Mining: Algorithms, Systems, Programming Models and Applications. 2012. p. 36–44.

Yang, H., Fong, S.. Incremental optimization mechanism for constructing a decision tree in data stream mining. Mathematical Problems in Engineering 2013;2013.

Yang, W., Wang, Z., Sun, C.. A collaborative representation based projections method for feature extraction. Pattern Recognition 2015;48(1):20–27.

Yu, K., Wang, L., Yu, Y.. Ordering-based kalman filter selective ensemble for classification. IEEE Access 2020;8:9715–9727.

Zhang, C., Liu, C., Zhang, X., Almpanidis, G.. An up-to-date comparison of state-of-the-art classification algorithms. Expert Systems with Applications 2017;82:128–150.

Zhang, T., Ramakrishnan, R., Livny, M.. Birch: an efficient data clustering method for very large databases. ACM sigmod record 1996;25(2):103–114.

Zhang, X., Xiao, H., Gao, R., Zhang, H., Wang, Y.. K-nearest neighbors rule combining prototype selection and local feature weighting for classification. Knowledge-Based Systems 2022;243:108451.

Zhang, Y., Cao, G., Wang, B., Li, X.. A novel ensemble method for k-nearest neighbor. Pattern Recognition 2019;85:13–25.

Zouggar, S.T., Adla, A.. A diversity-accuracy measure for homogenous ensemble selection. International Journal of Interactive Multimedia & Artificial Intelligence 2019;5(5).

FSC
www.fsc.org
MIX
Papier | Fördert gute Waldnutzung
FSC® C083411

Kolibri 360 GmbH
Ferdinand-Jühlke-Straße 7
99095 Erfurt, Deutschland
produktsicherheit@kolibri360.de

Druck:
CPI Druckdienstleistungen GmbH
im Auftrag der
Kolibri 360 GmbH
Ferdinand-Jühlke-Str. 7
99095 Erfurt